Entrepreneurship Centres

Gideon Maas • Paul Jones
Editors

Entrepreneurship Centres

Global Perspectives on their Contributions to Higher Education Institutions

Editors
Gideon Maas
International Centre for
 Transformational Entrepreneurship
Coventry University
Coventry, United Kingdom

Paul Jones
International Centre for
 Transformational Entrepreneurship
Coventry University
Coventry, United Kingdom

ISBN 978-3-319-47891-3   ISBN 978-3-319-47892-0 (eBook)
DOI 10.1007/978-3-319-47892-0

Library of Congress Control Number: 2016956863

© The Editor(s) (if applicable) and The Author(s) 2017
This book was advertised with a copyright holder in the name of the publisher in error, whereas the author holds the copyright.
This work is subject to copyright. All rights are solely and exclusively licensed by the Publisher, whether the whole or part of the material is concerned, specifically the rights of translation, reprinting, reuse of illustrations, recitation, broadcasting, reproduction on microfilms or in any other physical way, and transmission or information storage and retrieval, electronic adaptation, computer software, or by similar or dissimilar methodology now known or hereafter developed.
The use of general descriptive names, registered names, trademarks, service marks, etc. in this publication does not imply, even in the absence of a specific statement, that such names are exempt from the relevant protective laws and regulations and therefore free for general use.
The publisher, the authors and the editors are safe to assume that the advice and information in this book are believed to be true and accurate at the date of publication. Neither the publisher nor the authors or the editors give a warranty, express or implied, with respect to the material contained herein or for any errors or omissions that may have been made. The publisher remains neutral with regard to jurisdictional claims in published maps and institutional affiliations.

Cover illustration: Pattern adapted from an Indian cotton print produced in the 19th century

Printed on acid-free paper

This Palgrave Macmillan imprint is published by Springer Nature
The registered company is Springer International Publishing AG
The registered company address is: Gewerbestrasse 11, 6330 Cham, Switzerland

Preface

In the first book in the series on transformational entrepreneurship (Systemic Entrepreneurship – Contemporary Issues and Case Studies, 2015), the focus was on providing a broad overview of systemic (transformational) entrepreneurship. That book addressed the issues of low and slow socio-economic growth patterns and how a transformational approach can address this dilemma. It was highlighted that systemic entrepreneurship is about enabling change to how entrepreneurs and society act beyond local levels of entrepreneurial engagement.

This book uses the first book as a basis and explores how entrepreneurship centres can act as the kingpin within universities to stimulate transformational entrepreneurship. It is well known that entrepreneurship centres are the key leaders in universities stimulating enterprise and entrepreneurial activities. However, these important centres experience various challenges that sometimes cloud their focus and activities. In this book, the focus is on entrepreneurship centres and how they can play a meaningful role in transformational entrepreneurship. Principles of transformational entrepreneurship are combined with seven case studies from the UK, Spain, Canada and Ghana to illustrate the practical application of transformational entrepreneurship principles.

It is accepted that entrepreneurship centres operate in diverse communities, and therefore, a generalised approach on how these centres should organise themselves is not suggested. However, based on transformational principles and the seven case studies, this book ends off with various process questions that can guide interested people in creating an effective entrepreneurship centre or improving an existing centre. This book is not a 'how-to' guide for entrepreneurship centres – it is a critical reflection on how entrepreneurship centres can promote transformational entrepreneurship, which should result in sustainable socio-economic development.

Acknowledgements

Many people made this book possible. Firstly, the editors want to thank the leadership team of Coventry University who created the freedom and innovative space for the editors to explore principles and practices of transformational entrepreneurship. Secondly, the editors want to thank the various contributors of in order cases who are all noted individually within the 'Notes on Contributors' section. Lastly, the editors wish to thank Palgrave Macmillan which is undertaking this creative journey with us – we need more institutions like this!

Contents

Part I Introduction to Entrepreneurship Centres

1 An Overview of Transformation Entrepreneurship   3
  Gideon Maas and Paul Jones

2 The Role of Entrepreneurship Centres   11
  Gideon Maas and Paul Jones

Part II Cases of Entrepreneurship Centres within the UK

3 Coventry University   19
  Joan Lockyer

4 Lancaster University   41
  Fionnuala Schultz, Helen Fogg, Eleanor Hamilton
  and Sarah Jack

5 Scotland's Centres for Entrepreneurship (UK)   61
  Robert Smith

Part III European, Canadian and African Entrepreneurship Centres

6 EDEM Business School (Spain)   81
Martina Luckanicova and Andrea Conchado

7 Santander International Entrepreneurship Centre, University of Cantabria (Spain)   97
Federico Gutiérrez-Solana Salcedo, Inés Rueda Sampedro and Kerstin Maier

8 The Hunter Centre for Entrepreneurship and Innovation (Canada)   111
Simon Raby

9 Centre for Entrepreneurship and Small Enterprises Development, University of Cape Coast (Ghana)   125
Rosemond Boohene and Daniel Agyapong

Part IV Guidelines for Maintaining Sustainable Entrepreneurship Centres

10 Guidelines for Maintaining Sustainable Entrepreneurial Centres   143
Gideon Maas and Paul Jones

Index   153

About the Editors

Gideon Maas is the Director of the International Centre for Transformational Entrepreneurship and Professor of Professional Practice at Coventry University, UK. Gideon has broad international business and academic experiences in various countries. Within the academic environment, Gideon has created various entrepreneurship centres at different universities over the past years, developed and implemented undergraduate and postgraduate modules and programmes focusing specifically on enterprise and entrepreneurship. Recently, Gideon has created the Africa Institute for Transformational Entrepreneurship to assist African countries in supporting sustainable socio-economic growth. Gideon's research focus and experiences are in entrepreneurship, open innovation, growth strategies, entrepreneurial universities, implementation of entrepreneurial systems and family businesses. His research activities are industry and academic related, and he has published various books and articles in the public domain. Gideon is also currently a Visiting Professor at Anglia-Ruskin University and Vice President (Policy and Practice) of the Board of Trustees of the Institute of Small Business and Entrepreneurship.

Paul Jones is the Deputy Director of the International Centre for Transformational Entrepreneurship and Professor in Entrepreneurship at Coventry University. Prof Jones has worked in further and higher education for over 25 years. Prof Jones is an active researcher in the entrepreneurship discipline with 200-plus outputs including edited books (1), academic journals (49), book chapters (5), conference papers (103), working papers (11), reports (2) and research monographs (1) since 2002. Prof Jones is currently Editor-in-Chief of the *International Journal of Entrepreneurial Behaviour and Research* and Associate Editor of the *International Journal* of *Management Education*. In addition, Prof Jones has acted as a Guest Editor for several special issues including a special edition of the *Journal of Systems and Information Technology* examining the usage and impact of E-Business within the small business sector. In 2013, he was a Guest Editor for a special edition of the *Journal of Small Business and Enterprise Development* exploring international deployment examples of E-Business. In 2014, he acted as a Guest Editor for a special edition of *Education + Training* investigating the impact of e-learning and also as a Guest Editor for a special edition of the *International Journal of Management Education* exploring Entrepreneurial Education and its ability to implement change.

LIST OF ABBREVIATIONS

GEM	Global Entrepreneurship Monitor
HE	Higher Education
HEI	Higher Education Institutions
OECD	Organisation for Economic Co-operation and Development
QAA	Quality Assurance Agency
SME	Small- and Medium-Sized Enterprises
TEA	Total Early-Stage Entrepreneurial Activity
UK	United Kingdom

List of Figures

Fig. 3.1	The IAE model	25
Fig. 3.2	BA EE structure	33
Fig. 4.1	Overall research outputs within the W2GH programme until June 2015	54
Fig. 6.1	Marina de Empresas: Its pillars and main figures	83
Fig. 6.2	Domains of entrepreneurship education ecosystem	85
Fig. 6.3	Entrepreneurship education ecosystem in Marina de Empresas	86
Fig. 9.1	The three interrelated activities of CESED	130
Fig. 9.2	Flow chart of activities in CESED	134

LIST OF TABLES

Table 3.1	IAE student enrolment	29
Table 3.2	BA EE Recruitment	31
Table 3.3	The MA EEE structure	36
Table 4.1	Data on the North West of England	45
Table 6.1	Entrepreneurial activities in BBA and BSc	88
Table 6.2	Satisfaction in relation to the cross-curricular PBL activity: descriptive statistics	91
Table 6.3	Individual entrepreneurial orientation: descriptive statistics	93
Table 6.4	Progress in entrepreneurial orientation	94
Table 8.1	Key challenges experienced by a growing Entrepreneurship Centre	122
Table 10.1	Guiding questions for entrepreneurship centres	145

PART I

Introduction to Entrepreneurship Centres

CHAPTER 1

An Overview of Transformation Entrepreneurship

Gideon Maas and Paul Jones

Abstract It is argued that Higher Education Institutions (HEIs) can and should play an active role in supporting socio-economic development and the most effective strategy to achieve this is to adapt an entrepreneurial university philosophy. Furthermore, what is called for is a carefully constructed enterprising and entrepreneurship strategy which connects the corporate strategy of the HEI with operational activities. Such a strategy should take regional and institutional differences into consideration and therefore cannot be applied uniformly across all HEIs. One way to address this complexity of implementing enterprise and entrepreneurship activities within a HEI is to have a dedicated centre that can effectively implement such activities.

Keywords Entrepreneurship · Socio-economic development · HEIs · Innovation · Entrepreneurial eco-system

---

G. Maas (✉) · P. Jones
International Centre for Transformational Entrepreneurship, Coventry University, Coventry, United Kingdom
e-mail: gmaas@coventry.ac.uk; ac0359@coventry.ac.uk

© The Author(s) 2017
G. Maas, P. Jones (eds.), *Entrepreneurship Centres*,
DOI 10.1007/978-3-319-47892-0_1

1.1 Introduction

There are various ongoing global debates regarding the role of entrepreneurship within socio-economic development which includes areas such as the characteristics of an entrepreneur, the role of social entrepreneurship, and the policies that can assist entrepreneurship. The focus on creating contextualised and sustainable socio-economic development in countries and regions through the promotion of entrepreneurship further adds complications to the various debates. Several questions are raised during these debates such as whether policies and practices promoting entrepreneurship can be applied uniformly within a country or should it take regional differences into consideration? What type of entrepreneurship activity is required to create sustainable socio-economic development? Is the domain of entrepreneurial development not over politicised? What is the role of higher education institutions (HEIs) in the promotion of entrepreneurship?

The above questions illustrate a picture of complexity. However, in a knowledge driven world where innovation breeds further innovation it is important to clarify the questions to be answered. Only when the relevant questions are asked can academia, experts, industry and government start to investigate these questions and find deeper and meaningful clues stimulating sustainable socio-economic development. It is certainly not the intention of this book to answer all such questions but rather to focus on a specific issue namely the role of entrepreneurship centres in promoting contextualised and sustainable socio-economic development. In this regard, the editors embarked on a journey of discovery regarding the role of entrepreneurship centres within a rapidly evolving environment - an environment which calls for transformation in the way entrepreneurship development is approached. Therefore, before focusing on entrepreneurship centres specifically, it is important to reflect on the philosophy behind this initiative which is highlighted in this chapter.

1.2 Definitions

This book is not intended to be focused on theory alone – a hybrid approach is adopted where theory and applications will be discussed as mutually supporting concepts. In this regard, it is not the intention to debate the various definitions in detail. However, to guide readers in the use of important concepts the following definitions as they will apply in this book are as follows:

- **Enterprise**: the application of creative ideas and innovations to practical situations (QAA 2012: 8).
- **Entrepreneurship**: the application of enterprise skills specifically to creating and growing organisations in order to identify and build on opportunities (QAA 2012: 8).
- **Innovation**: it involves the utilisation of ideas in problem solving by developing processes and improving the way things are done by creating new products, services, processes and organisations (Dawson and Andriopoulos 2014).
- **Entrepreneurial eco-system**: a network of interconnected actors which formally and informally coalesce to connect, mediate, and govern the performance within the local entrepreneurial environment (Mason and Brown, OECD and Government of the Netherlands 2013).
- **Socio-economic growth**: a process that seeks to identify both the social and the economic needs within a community, and looks to create strategies that addresses those needs in ways that are practical and in the optimum interests of the community over the long term (Jaffee 1998).
- **Systemic entrepreneurship**: sub-systems interacting and collaborating to create a positive framework in which opportunities can be exploited; it should be socially productive and go beyond the local level (Sautet 2013).
- **Transformational entrepreneurship**: the creation of an innovative virtue-based organization for the purpose of shifting resources out of an area of lower into an area of higher purpose and greater value under conditions requiring a holistic perspective (Miller and Collier 2010).

1.3 THE CHANGING ROLE FOR HEIs

The global environment is characterised by various phenomena which not only influence businesses and Governments but also HEIs. The recent decision by the United Kingdom (UK) to exit the European Union will influence the way HEIs operate vis-à-vis their counterparts in Europe. Political unrest in some countries provides a restriction on the notion of academic freedom. Funding changes of HEIs influence them to reexamine their portfolio of programmes and services and how effectively they can optimise their activities. These changes force HEIs to revisit their business models i.e. some HEIs decided to follow a business model where they acknowledged the importance of entrepreneurship in socio-economic development and are actively involved in the process of promoting entrepreneurship. Some of these activities are performed by a dedicated Entrepreneurship Centre and in other examples entrepreneurial activity is part of the institution fabric of the HEI. The latter gave rise to the entrepreneurial university concept. The entrepreneurial university concept is best explained by NCEE (2010: 3) who indicates that it is a term that demonstrates *"how institutional leadership and a strong entrepreneurial culture can create the policies and practices that are conducive to the development of enterprising and entrepreneurial mind-sets and behaviours throughout the organisation – in management and administration, in teaching and research staff and in students and graduates"*. It is therefore accepted that entrepreneurial universities is well connected with the entrepreneurial eco-system making a significant contribution towards sustainable socio-economic development. Funding changes for HEIs can potentially create the problem of narrowing entrepreneurial focus on the commercialisation of ideas or small business start-ups alone. Such an approach can only be pursued if the starting point was a broad based approach to entrepreneurship i.e. where the initial focus is on enterprising skills, creating a positive attitude towards entrepreneurial behaviour and creation of entrepreneurial mind-sets.

Since entrepreneurship was introduced to UK HEIs, a plethora of initiatives were created such as entrepreneurial training programmes, venture creation degrees, acceleration of research focusing on a variety of entrepreneurship topics, creation of incubators and business parks, and provision of support services to new start-ups and existing entrepreneurs seeking business growth. Several national reports have also been published actively trying to guide and promote entrepreneurship development in HEIs (European Commission 2012; Wilson 2012; Witty 2013; Young 2014). These reports place different nuances on issues such as enterprise, entrepreneurship, innovation, and academia and business collaboration. HEIs therefore not only find themselves in a rapidly evolving environment but also need to reflect how they can effectively apply entrepreneurship within their institutions. This will be addressed in the following sections.

1.4 THE NEED FOR TRANSFORMATIONAL ENTREPRENEURSHIP

In a position paper on transformational entrepreneurship, Maas et al. (2016) suggested entrepreneurial activity which focuses predominantly on the individual entrepreneur or local region will typically not have the desired positive impact on national socio-economic development. Therefore, a balance should be struck between a focus on individual entrepreneurial activities and society-wide changes which may have a more positive impact on socio-economic growth. This shift in thinking from individual to countrywide conceptualisations of entrepreneurship or even from a dominant focus on micro-business start-ups to support of scalable businesses is not without its difficulties. It is without question that a focus on individual micro-business start-ups are far easier than constructing and implementing an eco-system allowing for transformation to occur on the socio-economic front and therefore not surprising that the latter are not well supported by universities. However, in order to address global phenomena (e.g. poverty, unemployment, low or no growth) transformation is required in the way entrepreneurship is supported as part of a total system i.e. a system consisting of individuals, the community, public sector, private sector, and natural resources. This broader approach emphasises the need for holistic thinking and in essence moves the concept of the entrepreneur from the individual to the context in which the individual is situated, that is to society more generally. This approach is not arguing against the existence of locally focused entrepreneurial activities, micro enterprises or subsistence enterprises; to the contrary, they are important for cascading wealth to the broader society. It is observed that various initiatives from Governments, HEIs and other support organisations exists which focuses on the micro-entrepreneurial level. What is argued for is an approach that will restore a balance between a micro and transformational orientation. The latter can be argued to be part of the domain of HEIs if their knowledge creation ability is taken into consideration. Policies and practices need to be devised to support this transformational approach. Marmer (2012) agrees that there is a current stalemate in terms of global socio-economic growth and that a new approach is called for. To bring about effective transformation, it is important to evaluate and challenge, when necessary, the heuristics upon which decisions are currently made. The danger of real time, tried and tested solutions (default heuristic) is that they can be short-term and policy driven. New approaches need to be devised that challenge default reactions and which create new frameworks for adaptive thinking.

1.5 ENTREPRENEURIAL ECO-SYSTEMS SUPPORTING TRANSFORMATIONAL ENTREPRENEURSHIP

In order to address transformational entrepreneurship, a supportive entrepreneurship eco-system should exist. In this regard, Roth and DiBella (2015: 7) state that "*Systemic change encompasses the enterprise, the larger set or system of organizations that depend upon each other and make improvements in ways that produce enduring rather than ephemeral value*". Mason and Brown (in OECD and the Government of the Netherlands, 2013: 1) agrees with the notion that an eco-system is a network of interconnected actors "*which formally and informally coalesce to connect, mediate, and govern the performance within the local entrepreneurial environment*". It is therefore essential that a clear perspective exist on who the role-players are within a specific context and what their focus of activities are. It can be argued that leaders in this eco-system need to create compelling narratives firstly in terms of what they want to achieve within a specific context, region or country. From this basis, a more focused entrepreneurial eco-system can be created to focus on growth opportunities and transforming societies. The existence of entrepreneurs, leaders, innovation and an entrepreneurial eco-system is by no means a guarantee that socio-economic development will be positively stimulated. These focus areas can create a positive environment for transformational entrepreneurship to flourish but can equally be a major stumbling block when policies are not supportive of such an environment or when policy makers simply rely on the past to predict the future. Furthermore, unproductive entrepreneurship (i.e. unlawful activities) flourishes because of a lack of rule-of-law. Even an over reliance on the provision of grants and subsidies may influence the creation of entrepreneurial mind-sets negatively i.e. it creates a dependency culture. Policies influencing the entrepreneurial eco-system should be investigated and tweaked, or in some cases radically changed, to support the entrepreneurial eco-system. Therefore, a careful analysis of the total eco-system is required which can guide finding optimal solutions for the current and future challenges facing socio-economic growth.

1.6 CONCLUSION

The above discussions might seem overly complex especially from a context where HEIs are not necessarily trained to be enterprising or entrepreneurial. What is required is a carefully constructed enterprising and entrepreneurship strategy which connects the corporate strategy of the HEI with more enterprising and entrepreneurial operational activities. Such a strategy should take regional and institutional differences into consideration and therefore cannot be applied uniformly across all HEIs. One way to address this complexity of implementing enterprise and entrepreneurship activities within a HEI is to have a dedicated centre that can spearhead these activities. This centre approach will be considered in the following chapters.

REFERENCES

Dawson, P., & Andriopoulos, C. (2014). *Managing change, creativity and innovation.* (2nd edition.) London: Sage Publication.

European Commission. (2012) Entrepreneurship 2020 Action Plan – Reigniting the entrepreneurial spirit in Europe. Brussels XXX, COM (2012) 795/2.

Jaffee, D. (1998). *Levels of socio-economic development theory.* London: Praeger.

Maas, G., Jones, P., & Lockyer, J. (2016) Position Paper: International Centre for Transformational Entrepreneurship, Coventry University, www.coventry.ac.uk/icte, 24 February 2016.

Marmer, M. (2012) Transformational Entrepreneurship: Where Technology Meets Societal Impact. Harvard Business Review, April 23.

Miller, R. A., & Collier, E. W. (2010). Redefining entrepreneurship: A virtues and values perspective. *Journal of Leadership, Accountability and Ethics, 8*(2), pages 80–89.

NCEE (2010) ENTREPRENEURIAL UNIVERSITY OF THE YEAR 2010 /2011. (2010) Available from http://ncee.org.uk/publications [15 April 2014]

OECD and Government of the Netherlands (2013) 'Entrepreneurial ecosystems and growth-orientated entrepreneurship – summary report of an international workshop', The Hague, 7 November 2013.

QAA. (2012) 'Enterprise and entrepreneurship education: Guidance for UK higher education providers', September 2012.

Roth, G. L., & DiBella, A. J. (2015). *Systemic change management – the five capabilities for improving enterprises.* New York: Palgrave MacMillan.

Sautet, F. (2013). Local and systemic entrepreneurship: Solving the puzzle of entrepreneurship and economic development. *Entrepreneurship Theory and Practice, 37*(2), 387–402.

Wilson, T. (2012), A Review of Business-University Collaboration [online] available from https://www.gov.uk/government/uploads/system/uploads/attachment_data/file/32383/12-610-wilson-review-business-university-collaboration.pdf. (accessed February 25th 2015).

Witty, A. (2013), Encouraging a British Invention Revolution: Sir Andrew Witty's Review of Universities and Growth [online] available from (accessed February 25th 2015)

Young, L. (2014) Enterprise for all: The relevance of Enterprise in Education. June 2014.

Gideon Maas is the Director of the International Centre for Transformational Entrepreneurship and Professor of Professional Practice at Coventry University, UK. Gideon has broad international business and academic experiences in various countries. Within the academic environment, Gideon has created various entrepreneurship centres at different universities over the past years, developed and implemented undergraduate and postgraduate modules and programmes focusing specifically on enterprise and entrepreneurship. Recently, Gideon has created the Africa Institute for Transformational Entrepreneurship to assist African countries in supporting sustainable socio-economic growth. Gideon's research focus and experiences are in entrepreneurship, open innovation, growth strategies, entrepreneurial universities, implementation of entrepreneurial systems and family businesses. His research activities are industry and academic related, and he has published various books and articles in the public domain. Gideon is also currently a Visiting Professor at Anglia-Ruskin University and Vice President (Policy and Practice) of the Board of Trustees of the Institute of Small Business and Entrepreneurship.

Paul Jones is the Deputy Director of the International Centre for Transformational Entrepreneurship and Professor in Entrepreneurship at Coventry University. Prof Jones has worked in further and higher education for over 25 years. Prof Jones is an active researcher in the entrepreneurship discipline with 200-plus outputs including edited books (1), academic journals (49), book chapters (5), conference papers (103), working papers (11), reports (2) and research monographs (1) since 2002. Prof Jones is currently Editor-in-Chief of the *International Journal of Entrepreneurial Behaviour and Research* and Associate Editor of the *International Journal of Management Education*. In addition, Prof Jones has acted as a Guest Editor for several special issues including a special edition of the *Journal of Systems and Information Technology* examining the usage and impact of E-Business within the small business sector. In 2013, he was a Guest Editor for a special edition of the *Journal of Small Business and Enterprise Development* exploring international deployment examples of E-Business. In 2014, he acted as a Guest Editor for a special edition of *Education + Training* investigating the impact of e-learning and also as a Guest Editor for a special edition of the *International Journal of Management Education* exploring Entrepreneurial Education and its ability to implement change.

CHAPTER 2

The Role of Entrepreneurship Centres

Gideon Maas and Paul Jones

Abstract The extant literature has focused on what entrepreneurship centres are doing or have done with minimal attention to considering their future role, especially within the context of transformational entrepreneurship. If it is accepted that entrepreneurship centres will continue to play an important role in the immediate future, then the question is whether the existing roles of entrepreneurship centres are in line with future expectations. There is a growing perspective that although a plethora of entrepreneurial support activities exist, they struggle to create the future desired state of socio-economic growth. Various questions are raised in this debate, such as the following: Are entrepreneurial centres part of the enterprising agenda or are they only used as a marketing or income-generating tool? If there is a definite role to play for entrepreneurship centres within a higher education institution's entrepreneurship agenda, what should their role be and what type of support should be provided to these entrepreneurship centres? These questions are addressed in this chapter.

Keywords Entrepreneurship centres · Transformational entrepreneurship · Strategic role · Resourcing · Structuring · Policy formation

---

G. Maas (✉) · P. Jones
International Centre for Transformational Entrepreneurship, Coventry University, Coventry, United Kingdom
e-mail: gmaas@coventry.ac.uk; ac0359@coventry.ac.uk

2.1 Introduction

It would be an ideal environment where the higher education institution's (HEI's) fabric is such that a dedicated centre is not needed to stimulate enterprise and entrepreneurship activity. However, it is the experience of the editors that such an ideal situation does not exist and that in most cases HEIs need a dedicated centre to stimulate enterprise and entrepreneurship activities. Finkle et al. (2013) mooted that it is accepted that much of the entrepreneurial activities within HEIs can be attributed to the existence of an entrepreneurship centre. Despite this entrepreneurship centres tend to experience various challenges such as a lack of resources and a diverse set of expectations. This expectation from multi-stakeholders has led some entrepreneurship centres to undertake a variety of activities to survive and to address multi-stakeholder expectations that they tend to lose focus. This loss in focus is not only influencing HEI's activities but also may have a detrimental impact on sustainable socio-economic development of regions. Deduced from this discussion, the aim of this chapter is to reflect on the current research, practices and roles of entrepreneurship centres.

2.2 Overview of Entrepreneurship Centres

A search of research focusing on the role of entrepreneurship centres in the global environment revealed limited research in the role that entrepreneurship centres can play in stimulating sustainable socio-economic growth through transformational entrepreneurship. However, extant research suggests that there is no doubt that entrepreneurship centres can and should play an important role in stimulating enterprise and entrepreneurship activities within HEIs (Finkle et al. 2006, 2013; Nelles and Vorley 2011).

Within an entrepreneurial university context, it cannot merely be accepted that all students are enterprising and entrepreneurial. However, it is accepted that students should be exposed to entrepreneurial learning and through that achieve the goal of encouraging an individual's intention to act enterprising and/or entrepreneurially. Such activities should not be the sole responsibility of an entrepreneurship centre within HEIs. Entrepreneurship centres should play a direct (e.g. presenting their own programmes and activities) and indirect role (e.g. undertake joint programmes/activities with other faculties) in promoting enterprise and entrepreneurship activities.

Despite their successes, entrepreneurship centres experience various challenges such as limited and variability of resources, high and diverse expectations from various stakeholders, a diverse set of internal and external constituencies, finding appropriate staff, developing legitimacy within the HEI framework, faculty jealousy and lack of effective measuring of success (Finkle et al. 2006, 2013). Within this context, the goals of entrepreneurship centres vary significantly between new firm creation, researching market opportunities, developing enterprising and entrepreneurship skills among students and staff, and contributing to the capitalisation of knowledge (Del-Palacio et al. 2008). However, it can be accepted that the aims of entrepreneurship centres should be different if their strategies are in line with regional realities. Maas et al. (2015) agree that entrepreneurship centres differ in size and that some centres provide all-inclusive services from knowledge creation to incubation and growth support activities and other centres focus specifically on knowledge transfer, leaving the incubation and growth activities to other departments or science and technology parks. However, what they also discovered is that the majority of entrepreneurship centres agree that there is an overall HEI strategy that guides their activities, although they are not always clear on how it guides their activities. That brings into question the strategic importance a HEI attached to enterprise and entrepreneurship activities.

The positioning of entrepreneurship centres within HEI's structure varies significantly, for example, some are located within business schools, others function independently from faculties, whilst some are located in career advice services (Maas and Jones, 2015). The location is linked to the HEI's corporate strategy, for example, at Coventry University (UK) the corporate strategy is that of an entrepreneurial university and therefore the entrepreneurship centre is located independently from faculties. It is assumed that when an entrepreneurship centre is part of a specific faculty or department the goals of such a faculty and department would be pursued. The research of Maas et al. (2015) also indicated the variety of models in terms of the location of entrepreneurship centres. However, it seems that a higher priority is attached to an entrepreneurship centre that is multidisciplinary, interdisciplinary and accessible by all faculties within a HEI. This is supported by Thorp and Goldstein (2010: 31), who maintained that "*a culture that accepts and promotes interdisciplinary work within the traditional disciplines and across traditional barriers will have a greater impact*" than free-standing units promoting such interdisciplinary activities. The editors agree with Thorp and Goldstein (2010) but maintain that the current culture within HEIs is not conducive to an integrated approach and requires entrepreneurship centres to steer the development of enterprise and entrepreneurship agenda from within a HEI.

Following the trend that entrepreneurship centres can achieve more if they do not belong to a specific faculty or department, it can also be reasoned that such centres should be the guardians of the entrepreneurial ecosystem within HEIs. Within HEIs, such an entrepreneurial ecosystem can be interpreted as collaborative and holistic activities focusing on the promotion of entrepreneurial mindsets, which is guided by a clear institutional strategy. The formalised HEI entrepreneurial ecosystem guided by a transparent institutional strategy can address the acceptance and legitimacy of enterprise and entrepreneurship within HEIs (Maas and Jones, 2015). A set of carefully formulated policies, procedures and practices should guide the implementation of an entrepreneurial ecosystem at HEIs.

Finding and keeping the right staff is a major problem for entrepreneurship centres. One challenge is the pathways to promotion – entrepreneurially orientated staff might deviate from the normal pathways required for promotion for academic staff (Clarysse et al. 2011). To retain suitably qualified staff within entrepreneurship centres therefore demands a different approach to promotion and remuneration. Within such an approach, it should still be possible for staff to be promoted to professorial levels because of their contributions although it might be different from the pathway for a normal academic person. Staff profiles may therefore be different with less academic and more business experience and evidence of opportunistic and risk-tolerant behaviour.

Within entrepreneurship centres, a variety of activities are found which include new firm creation, market research, skills development, motivating entrepreneurial behaviour, entrepreneurship knowledge creation and improving the social welfare of the community in which the HEI operates. The study of Maas et al. (2015) confirmed the variety or activities, which were derived from the corporate strategy, or, alternatively, a lack of clarity about the corporate strategy. The development of enterprise and entrepreneurship skills is perceived as their most important priority with a low priority attached to research specifically focusing on policy matters. It is therefore no wonder that entrepreneurship centres indicated that the most important priority is assisting the development of enterprise and entrepreneurship curriculum followed by the actual delivering of specific modules and programmes.

Lastly, entrepreneurship centres experience challenges regarding financial resources. A lack of clarity about what the role of entrepreneurship centres is within HEIs can lead to insecurity regarding financial resources. Furthermore, the way entrepreneurship centres are measured in terms of success might further influence the way resources are made available to these centres. If measurement is according to financial contributions, a lack of success in this regard can influence the longevity of such a centre. However, if the entrepreneurship centre is linked to the corporate strategy of the HEI, it can be accepted that measurement should include reputational gains as well, which is not always directly quantifiable.

2.3 CONCLUSION

Entrepreneurship centres can and still should play a strategic role in promoting enterprise and entrepreneurship activities within the near future. What is important in this role of entrepreneurship centres is that it should be clearly linked to the HEI's corporate strategy for enterprise and entrepreneurship. Within this regard, the structuring and resourcing of entrepreneurship centres should follow this strategy. It might be seen that entrepreneurship centres are opportunist in finding new sources of resources to survive financially but that can have a detrimental impact on the focus of their activities. This might be the reason why policy formulation is not high on the agenda of entrepreneurship centres because it can be perceived as too cost intensive.

REFERENCES

Clarysse, B., Tartari, V. & Salter, A. 2011. The impact of entrepreneurial capacity, experience and organizational support on academic entrepreneurship. *Research Policy 40*(2011), 1084–1093.

Del-Palacio, I., Sole, F. & Batista-Foguet, M. (2008). University entrepreneurship centres as service businesses. *The Service Industries Journal*, *28*(7), 939–951.

Finkle, T., Kuratko, D. F. & Goldsby, M. G. (2006). An examination of entrepreneurship centres in the United States: A national survey. *Journal of Small Business Management*, *44*(2), 184–206.

Finkle, T. A., Menzies, T. V., Kuratko, D. F. & Goldsby, M. G. (2013). An examination of the financial challenges of entrepreneurship centers throughout the world. *Journal of Small Business and Entrepreneurship*, *26*(1), 67–85.

Maas, G., Jones, P. & Lloyd Reason, L. (2015) Centres for Entrepreneurship at a cross road – Quo Vadis, 38th Institute for Small Business and Entrepreneurship conference, Technology and Innovation Centre, Glasgow, UK 11–12th November, ISBN: 978-1-900862-28-8.

Maas, G., & Jones, P. (2015). *Systemic entrepreneurship – Contemporary issues and case studies*. London: Palgrave Macmillan.
Nelles, J., & Vorley, T. (2011). Entrepreneurial architecture: A blueprint for entrepreneurial universities. *Canadian Journal of Administrative Sciences, 28*, 341–353.
Thorp, H., & Goldstein, B. (2010). *Engines of innovation – The entrepreneurial university in the twenty-first century*. Chapel Hill: The University of North Carolina Press.

Gideon Maas is the Director of the International Centre for Transformational Entrepreneurship and Professor of Professional Practice at Coventry University, UK. Gideon has broad international business and academic experiences in various countries. Within the academic environment, Gideon has created various entrepreneurship centres at different universities over the past years, developed and implemented undergraduate and postgraduate modules and programmes focusing specifically on enterprise and entrepreneurship. Recently, Gideon has created the Africa Institute for Transformational Entrepreneurship to assist African countries in supporting sustainable socio-economic growth. Gideon's research focus and experiences are in entrepreneurship, open innovation, growth strategies, entrepreneurial universities, implementation of entrepreneurial systems and family businesses. His research activities are industry and academic related, and he has published various books and articles in the public domain. Gideon is also currently a Visiting Professor at Anglia-Ruskin University and Vice President (Policy and Practice) of the Board of Trustees of the Institute of Small Business and Entrepreneurship.

Paul Jones is the Deputy Director of the International Centre for Transformational Entrepreneurship and Professor in Entrepreneurship at Coventry University. Prof Jones has worked in further and higher education for over 25 years. Prof Jones is an active researcher in the entrepreneurship discipline with 200-plus outputs including edited books (1), academic journals (49), book chapters (5), conference papers (103), working papers (11), reports (2) and research monographs (1) since 2002. Prof Jones is currently Editor-in-Chief of the *International Journal of Entrepreneurial Behaviour and Research* and Associate Editor of the *International Journal of Management Education*. In addition, Prof Jones has acted as a Guest Editor for several special issues including a special edition of the *Journal of Systems and Information Technology* examining the usage and impact of E-Business within the small business sector. In 2013, he was a Guest Editor for a special edition of the *Journal of Small Business and Enterprise Development* exploring international deployment examples of E-Business. In 2014, he acted as a Guest Editor for a special edition of *Education + Training* investigating the impact of e-learning and also as a Guest Editor for a special edition of the *International Journal of Management Education* exploring Entrepreneurial Education and its ability to implement change.

PART II

Cases of Entrepreneurship Centres within the UK

The changing environment and its impact on universities and entrepreneurship centres were discussed in Chapters 1 and 2. In Part II of this book, two case studies of universities in England (Coventry University and Lancaster University) and a case study of an entrepreneurship centre in Scotland are presented. All three are based in regions with unique characteristics, which resulted in applying different solutions to opportunities and challenges. Therefore, readers should consider the first two chapters when reading the cases determining how adjustments were made over time. Specific areas to identify in the following three case studies are as follows:

- Coventry University (Chapter 3): how leadership and strategic changes influenced the strategic direction of the entrepreneurship centre; how the centre is positioned outside faculties; the development of a new focus.
- Lancaster University (Chapter 4): how an institute for entrepreneurship migrated into a department within a business school; the various academic programmes presented with a balanced approach between theory and practice.
- Scottish entrepreneurship centres (Chapter 5): the role of experts in the promotion of entrepreneurship; the importance of a wider ecosystem in promoting entrepreneurship; can a specific regional focus be promoted in entrepreneurship.

Within the three case studies presented, it is clear that the regional and institutional strategies play a meaningful role in the way entrepreneurship centres operate. It is furthermore clear that in some situations these centres are prone to budget decisions that are not always in line with a broader strategic approach in the promotion of entrepreneurship. Despite these challenges, the three case studies highlighted best practices in terms of education, research and extracurricular activities. What is clear from these best practices is that entrepreneurship centres need to play a university-wide role, they need to focus on impact which would probably be external to the university, the need for succession planning of qualified staff that should populate these centres and that these centres should be part of a wider entrepreneurial ecosystem internal and external to universities. Lastly, it can be observed that most of the entrepreneurship centres are doing more or less the same and therefore a call for differentiation is probably just.

CHAPTER 3

Coventry University

Joan Lockyer

Abstract The Coventry University (CU) case study illustrates how entrepreneurship is promoted through the Institute of Applied Entrepreneurship (IAE) which became the International Centre for Transformational Entrepreneurship (ICTE). ICTE is a natural evolution of the response of CU to changes internal and external to the university. Therefore, the case study will explore the rationale for the approach adopted at CU and provide an overview of the programmes offered by the IAE and now ICTE.

Keywords Leadership · Expansion · CU · Entrepreneur development · Venture creation

3.1 Introduction

The Institute of Applied Entrepreneurship (IAE) was formed in 2008 through the merger of a number of disparate activities which ran across the university to support its burgeoning enterprise and entrepreneurship agenda. In 2015, the IAE academic team merged with the newly formed

---

J. Lockyer (✉)
International Centre for Transformational Entrepreneruship, Coventry University, Coventry, UK
e-mail: aa7114@coventry.ac.uk

© The Author(s) 2017
G. Maas, P. Jones (eds.), *Entrepreneurship Centres*,
DOI 10.1007/978-3-319-47892-0_3

International Centre for Transformational Entrepreneurship (ICTE). ICTE might be considered a natural evolution of the IAE and is a response to the stage of development of enterprise and entrepreneurship at Coventry University. Moreover, a change in leadership at the university in 2014 heralded a new era in the university's remit and strategy. Under the new leadership, the focus shifted to a more research and teaching orientation, with clearer lines of demarcation between its commercial and academic activities. This being the case the IAE needed to be reformed, and in August 2015, ICTE was launched. This case study will discuss the IAE as an enterprise and entrepreneurship centre and its subsequent merger into ICTE. To set the context for this discussion, the case study will explore the rationale for the approach adopted at Coventry University and provide an overview of the programmes offered by the IAE and now ICTE.

3.2 Coventry University

CU has long aspired to be recognised as a Globally Entrepreneurial University. Enterprise and entrepreneurship are core values within the business and strategic plans and are key themes in all aspects of the university's endeavours. The IAE was established to further these aspirations nationally and internationally and it was frequently presented to the external world as the university's face of enterprise and entrepreneurship.

To understand the context in which CU's operates, it is important to understand its antecedence, and this goes back to 1843 when it was Coventry College of Design. It later became Coventry School of Arts (1852), then the Municipal School of Arts (1902) and eventually the College of Arts in 1954. In 1970, the College of Arts merged with Lanchester College of Technology and Rugby College of Engineering to become Lanchester Polytechnic; named in honour of a famous local automotive industry pioneer, Dr Frederick Lanchester. This merger of science and art, in the form of creativity and innovation, is still the bedrock of the Coventry approach.

Whilst Frederick Lanchester was renowned locally, Lanchester Polytechnic was a hard place to locate outside the region and so in 1987 the name was changed to Coventry Polytechnic. Changes in UK legislation in 1992 allowed polytechnics to become universities and so CU was formed. A major expansion of the university came in 1998 when the CU Technology Park was established. The operational management of the

Park was provided by Coventry University Enterprises (CUE), the trading arm of CU Higher Education Corporation. The Technology Park was partly intended as an incubator for small businesses and also as the home for a number of the university's commercial subsidiaries; one of which eventually was the IAE.

Additional expansion of the university commenced in 2005, and this coincided with a decision to focus more of the energies and resources on research activities. The focus on research, amongst other things, has resulted in Coventry being the first of the former polytechnics to break into the top thirty universities (Guardian University Guide, 2015). A further £100 million investment in research, and the infrastructure to support it, is pledged as part of the strategic plan to 2021. This investment is intended to create about eleven new research centres, all of which will carry out research that has a 'real world' impact. The investment is testament to its strong commercial focus and its research ambitions.

The current Vice-Chancellor (VC) of CU Prof John Latham, in his previous role as Director of CUE, was instrumental in the development of the Technology Park. John Latham is also a graduate of CU. He argues that while universities "*have a public ethos, [and] they're publicly controlled, you're trying to run several commercial subsidiaries and trying to make sure that you've got international activities*" (*Kim Thomas, Guardian*, 2014). Furthermore, he argues that "*the only way to do ground breaking research is to be more commercial in parts of our group's activities*" (ibid). Following this ethos, CU's business model utilises surplus funds, generated by its commercial subsidiaries and donated to the university as a charitable gift, to support its research and expansion activities. The commercial arm of the University Group, he argues, allows the academic arm to function and grow (ibid).

An additional expansion in the university's services has been through the establishment of CU London Campus which opened in 2005 and attracts mostly international students. In addition, CU College was founded in 2012 and offers a 'no frills' model of education of part-time professional and vocational courses, with a fee structure substantially below that of the university. Its demographic and working patterns are designed for students who need more flexible access to higher education, such as evenings and weekend classes.

The World Economic Forum report on 'Educating the Next Wave of Entrepreneurs: Unlocking entrepreneurial capabilities to meet the global challenges of the 21st Century' (World Economic Forum 2009) argues that entrepreneurship education is essential for developing the human capital necessary for the society of the future. The report says,

> ... it is not enough to add entrepreneurship on the perimeter – it needs to be core to the way education operates. Educational institutions, at all levels (primary, secondary and higher education) need to adopt 21st century methods and tools to develop the appropriate learning environment for encouraging creativity, innovation and the ability to 'think out of the box' to solve problems. This requires a fundamental rethinking of educational systems, both formal and informal, as well as the way in which teachers or educators are trained, how examination systems function and the way in which rewards, recognition and incentives are given. (World Economic Forum 2009: 9)

The approach to enterprise and entrepreneurship education at CU generally, and in particular in the IAE very much embodies these sentiments.

3.3 Institute of Applied Entrepreneurship

There are a number of reasons why IAE was established in 2008. The VC at that time believed that an institute to promote the entrepreneurial credentials of the university was a necessity. The IAE was positioned in CUE as one of its commercial subsidiaries and was located on the Technology Park. Given the Park's focus on supporting small- and medium-sized enterprises (SMEs) and incubating start-up companies, it was a logical option.

The establishment of entrepreneurship centres in universities had been an increasingly common feature since the late 1990s (Kretz and Creso 2013; Finkle et al. 2006, 2012), and so in some respects the formation of the IAE was a little late in both European (see Shattock's "Review of Entrepreneurialism in Universities", 2009) and American terms (see Finkle et al.'s "An examination of entrepreneurship centres in the United States", 2006). However, with respect to trends in the UK, it was still relatively unusual to have a specialist centre for entrepreneurship in a university at this time. As Shattock's (2009) study indicates, the structure of the institution is a key factor and in particular the role of the VC as a driver for change. CU's entrepreneurial mission and strategy had started to emerge at this time under a VC committed to the creation of a 'Globally Entrepreneurial University' and a director of CUE who could see the benefit of locating such a centre in that part of the Group's activities. In addition, at the time of the creation of the IAE, the university was seeing an increased interest in entrepreneurship from existing and new students. Internal research suggested that many students has already started a businesses (maybe trading online); others had expressed an interest in starting a business at some point.

Whilst CU's ambitions were shifting towards a more research-orientated focus, this was at a very early stage. Therefore in the wider context, the establishment of the IAE resonates with what Kretz and Creso (2013) describe as a mechanism for dealing with universities with limited contribution to economic growth. Unlike research-intensive universities, they argue, where the expectation is that research and innovation will provide economic benefits, the response from more applied universities has been in *"the decision.... to support student entrepreneurship [as a] realistic response to such limitations"* (2013, 503). They suggest that for *"universities lacking expansive research infrastructure and star-faculty to promote local economic engagement"* (2013, 503) a viable alternative strategy is supporting student entrepreneurship. CU may be seen as fitting this pattern at that time; however, there was substantial outreach through CUE's activities. In reality, the IAE's function was threefold: (1) to generate third-stream income, (2) to fulfil a local engagement and outreach function and (3) to provide students with the support they needed to start a business. Running alongside this agenda was a pan-university strategy to support employability. This agenda started in 2006 and involved the delivery of a series of elective modules under the banner of the Add+Vantage initiative. Over 150 × 10 credit modules were developed and were made compulsory for all undergraduates. A number of enterprise and entrepreneurship modules formed part of this portfolio.

Before the formation of the IAE, business support and enterprise training was provided by a range of different entities. For example, the Add+Vantage enterprise and entrepreneurship modules were developed and delivered by the Business Enterprise Support Team (BEST), which was attached to Business Development Support Office – a CU-based activity. The BEST team was transformed into the Student Enterprise Centre (SEC) and, together with the Business Enterprise Works (BEW) (a CUE-based activity), provided start-up support and mentoring to students, staff and external SMEs. When the IAE was formed, SEC and BEW were incorporated into it providing a single coherent vehicle offering business support activities and enterprise and entrepreneurship education. The enterprise and entrepreneurship Add+Vantage modules were transferred to the IAE; in addition, it developed a BA in Enterprise and Entrepreneurship (BA EE) and a range of Continuing Progressional Development (CPD) and postgraduate programmes, all of which are discussed in detail later.

This newly constructed team of 'hybrids' – business support professionals (previously attached to other initiatives across the university) and academics with a depth of business experience – constituted the new IAE. Because the institute was located in CUE, it was located on the Technology Park which is just outside the city centre ring road. However, because the academic arm (CU) is located within the ring road, the IAE frequently referred to itself as working on 'both sides of the ring road'. This was more than just an arbitrary geographical reference. The team perceived a mindset difference between these domains which is needed to negotiate.

Once the merger of the various groups that formed the IAE was established, it became clear that a formal well-contextualised conceptual model was needed which could act as a basis for the further acceleration of entrepreneurial activities in a planned and integrated manner. The model in Fig. 3.1 was created and launched during December 2010.

The model aimed to visually represent the various component parts of the IAE and show that strong and strategic links could be created through them to promote a version of entrepreneurship that was institutionally unique. At the core of the model (1) is the basic remit of the IAE, that being to promote entrepreneurship, an entrepreneurial culture and personal development. This was underpinned with knowledge, innovation and research (2) and supported through mentoring, finance and networking (3). Above the core activities the model identifies how support could be accessed (4). Linked to each is a range of project examples that IAE staff engaged in to support (and fund) delivery (5). Personal and business growth form the axises of the model.

The ambition of the IAE conceptual model was to create the framework to support a lifestyle of entrepreneurship which could be achieved through focusing on the *personal development* of the entrepreneur and on providing the *entrepreneurial* and *business skills* needed to exploit and implement new ideas. The IAE believed that all three areas needed to be in harmony in order to create sustainable success and improved socio-economic growth. This model also recognises that support should be

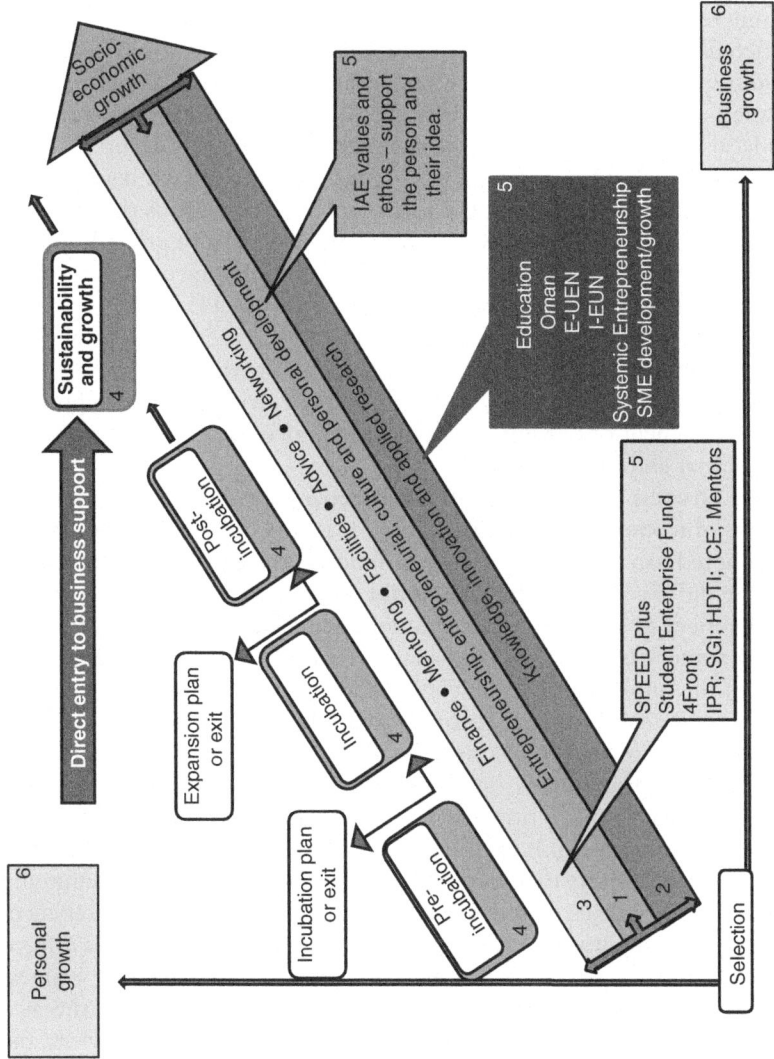

Fig. 3.1 The IAE model

tailored to the specific needs of a person and business and to accommodate change as the person/business progressed through different phases, namely obtaining knowledge, pre-incubation, incubation and commercialisation.

Because the IAE operated in both CUE and CU, it could access the various specialist units within the University Group to support the model; creating a one-stop service for existing and potential entrepreneurs. The model also acknowledged that the measurement of entrepreneurial success was changing. No longer was it only input driven (e.g. how many people were trained and supported), the focus was moving towards the potential and real impact of entrepreneurs on the environment (e.g. are the businesses that were supported still in existence and growing). This approach was in reality the seed that would later emerge as ICTE.

Since its introduction, this conceptual model has acted as a focal point for various activities undertaken by the IAE and the wider CU group, such as bidding and revisiting the entrepreneurship curriculum, and supported the development of new initiatives including focus on systemic and transformational entrepreneurship.

The business model of the IAE was dependent upon various revenue streams. Income came primarily from teaching. IAE staff also ran or contributed to a number of European-funded projects. While involvement in these did not generate income, it did cover costs. It also supported the development of the IAE brand. Brand building was important as the IAE was in some ways in a 'no man's land' between the wholly commercial parts of the university and the wholly academic.

The range of European projects that the IAE participated in was impressive, but caused resource challenges. Little time remained to develop new programmes or to capitalise on the potential for research and publications. In addition, there was pressure to make a contribution to centre (CU) from surplus revenue. This at times exacerbated the resource limitations as projects that were not ideally suited to the IAE's remit and aspirations were taken to secure additional income. For some members of the IAE, teaching was the main focus. As the range of programmes offered increased, the necessity to pull away from some aspects of external business support and project engagement also increased. While most of the academic team could teach and undertake a range of consultancy services, the business support staff could not teach. An imbalance progressively emerged between academic and non-academic staff, and this resulted in some tensions.

3.4 Teaching and Learning

Various programmes have been offered by the IAE since its inception and most continue to be part of the ICTE portfolio, which are

- BA in Enterprise and Entrepreneurship
- MA in Global Entrepreneurship (MA GE)
- MA in Enterprise and Entrepreneurship Education (MA EEE)

A number of CPD programmes have been offered at the professional or postgraduate level in areas such as leadership, strategy, social entrepreneurship, family business management and succession planning. Insufficient time on the whole was the reason that these programmes progressively dropped from the portfolio.

The Add+Vantage modules have provided a consistent source of revenue for the IAE and now to ICTE. When they were originally developed, BA EE utilised many of them as part of its programme offer so it makes sense to discuss them first.

Add+Vantage Modules

The Add+Vantage range of employability modules were first launched in 2005/2006. As part of this 150-module offer, the BEST contributed a range of about 16 modules on enterprise and entrepreneurship, and when BEST became part of the IAE, these modules came with them.

The Add+Vantage modules were designed to achieve three main objectives

- Provide students with an opportunity to choose additional modules to improve their employability prospects
- Provide structured support to help develop student's career management skills through an online Employability Learning Programme (ELP)
- Provide students with the opportunity to improve their employability competencies, such as adaptability, decisiveness and initiative

Students were expected to take one 10-credit module (5 CATS) each year; it could be in either semester 1 or 2. They had to pass these modules to progress. The modules were assessed through a series of components – a group presentation, a 500-word reflective statement and a subject-specific 1,500-word essay – and through the creation of an ELP webfolio.

The modules aimed to make CU students standout with employers by ensuring that they were 'work ready' on completion of their degree programme. However, it is probably fair to say that the modules were disliked by many students. They found the disconnection with their main subject too great. The attendance levels were poor, so was their engagement with the material (in particular, the ELP), and there was a range of technology issues. Staff were equally initially frustrated with the programme. There was a high level of bureaucracy. Assignments, with several components, had to be set, marked, moderated and reviewed by external examiners. The attendance issues, coupled with link between passing the module in order to proceed, added to the burden.

However, for the IAE, the Add+Vantage modules formed an important part of the way in which the institute engaged with the wider university. The IAE's modules attracted students from all faculties in approximately the following proportions: 10 % from the Faculty of Humanities and Art, 59 % from the Faculty of Business and Law, 20 % from the Faculty of Engineering and Computing and 11 % from the Faculty of Health and Life Sciences. So, while the IAE experienced many of the problems outlined earlier, the Add+Vantage programme did serve a number of useful purposes; revenue generation being not the least.

Although they have gone through a number of changes, refinements and improvements, the Add+Vantage modules are still part of all CU programmes. In fact, they were identified as an example of good practice during the 2015 QAA, Higher Education Review of CU. This in a way shows that the university is not afraid to experiment and to change if required.

The number of students attracted to the IAE modules continued to grow steadily year on year. Table 3.1 is a rough approximation of the number of students who have elected to take IAE modules since 2006.

The range of Add+Vantage modules offered by the IAE has also evolved over that time, some examples are Introduction to Entrepreneurship, Social Media for Business, Business Start-Up, Hi-Tech Entrepreneurship and Getting a Job – What Employers Want from You.

Table 3.1 IAE student enrolment

2006/ 2007	2007/ 2008	2008/ 2009	2009/ 2010	2010/ 2011	2011/ 2012	2012/ 2013	2013/ 2014	2014/ 2015	2015/ 2016
495	696	770	758	990	1,014	1,133	1,193	1,220	1,725
41 FTE	58 FTE	64 FTE	63 FTE	82 FTE	85 FTE	94 FTE	99 FTE	101 FTE	143 FTE

Note: FTE, Full Time Equivalent.

BA in Enterprise and Entrepreneurship

BA EE is often presented as a flagship programme for both the IAE (now ICTE) and the university. It is described as a Venture Creation Programme (VCP) and is one of only a small number of VCPs operating at undergraduate level in the UK (www://chalmers.se/vcplist). The concept of the VCP emerged from an Entrepreneurial Learning Forum that took place at Chalmers University, Sweden, in 2012, where the founders or current leaders of VCPs came together to share their knowledge, learning and experience of setting up and running such programmes (ibid.). Lackeus argues that "*venture creation programmes could be regarded as a bridge between a knowledge producing academic and value creation processes in society at large*" (2013: 2). Lackeus further notes that the adopted approaches, variously described as action-based, effectual, experiential, blur the boundaries between the formal and non-formal learning environment. In many ways they represent the epitome of entrepreneurship education in that they are designed to support business start-up as part of the core aims of the programme; their express intention being that students should complement their studies (undergraduate or postgraduate) with a viable business to work in and grow (Lockyer and Adams 2014).

Globally, various approaches are adopted to the establishment of higher education programmes that support venture creation and many of the VCPs are run by specialist enterprise centres, which are not part of a university business school, the IAE is one example. According to Morris, this is based on the belief that entrepreneurship is essentially experiential (Morris et al. 2011). Business school models tend to be more traditionally aligned with managerialist (or causal) thinking based on the extent to which it is believed the future can be predicted and controlled (Sarasvathy 2001a, b: 6). While rule-based systems, such as universities, like the certainty of causal thinking, they also understand that effectual thinking, with its inbuilt serendipity, has the potential to create more impactful entrepreneurial outcomes (Lockyer and Adams 2014).

Given the complexity of these programmes, it is perhaps not surprising that there are so few VCPs available to undergraduates. They are expensive to run, time consuming, require a range of specialist business and academic skills and pose a real challenge to students. The number of students typically attracted to these programmes is low, generally between 10 and 25 per year; so staff/student ratios are very high. One reason for this may be that the process of venture creation is 'messy', that is, it is non-linear and draws upon knowledge, skills, competencies and emotion. Schindehutte et al. (2006) in particular draw upon the last component, that of emotion, as being one of the main characteristics of the experiential base. They argue that although rational decision-making is important, in some situations reliance on effectual or emotional thinking is a quicker and easier way to navigate uncertainty (Schindehutte et al. 2006, 350).

Although it would not be referred to as a VCP at that time, in 2007 the university set up the BA Business Enterprise (BABE) with the express intention of supporting student business start-up as part of their degree programme. The BABE was located in the Business School (BS). In 2007, the name was changed to BA in Enterprise and Entrepreneurship and it was brought under the control of the IAE, but its Faculty home was still the BS. However, although intended as primarily an entrepreneurship-focused programme, the BA EE was actually a hybrid programme comprised of BS and IAE modules, broadly on a 50/50 ratio. The reason for this was largely pragmatic as the number of students was low and the programme was only viable on that basis. The IAE has no input to the content or delivery of the BS modules or their assessment. The modules taken by BS EE students from the BS portfolio were open to a wide range of programmes and therefore in many respects were generic and not entirely appropriate to the IAE's needs.

In 2010, a proposal was made and accepted to move the BA EE programme entirely under the control of the IAE for the next intake (2011), whilst leaving current students largely on the existing programme as it was phased out. This phased introduction of the programme suited both the current students, who had become accustomed to large group teaching, and the IAE as it allowed time to increase staffing resources and to assess the methodology adopted with a new group of students. By this stage, the IAE had moved its Faculty home to the School of Lifelong Learning (SLL). It was felt that the SLL had more relevance to the nature of the programme than the BS. There has been some resistance to the

Table 3.2 BA EE Recruitment

Academic Year	Level 1	Level 2	Level 3	Comments
Original Programme				Delivered by the Business School
2006	10			
2007	10	11		
2008	12	10	7	Joint delivery with IAE
2009	21	10	8	
2010	21	15	11	
2011	-	17	11	Programme revised, level 2/3 being phased out
2012	-	-	13	Last year of old programme
New Programme				
2011	29	-	-	New programme phased in
2012	17	26	-	
2013	11	11	26	First full programme completed
2014	15	9	12	Placement student returned for third year.
2015	25	14	9	More support with recruitment and admissions
2016	N/A	19	N/A	Data not available (N/A)

approaches to teaching adopted by the IAE and as its faculty home, the BS effectively had the power to veto proposed revisions.

Table 3.2 shows recruitment for the BA EE from 2006 to 2015 and the retention figures year on year. The coloured blocks show the progression pathways for the students and the retention rates.

This table highlights both the low recruitment numbers relative to other programmes and the relatively high attrition rate. This is not uncommon for VCP programmes. Several factors contribute to this:

- In terms of recruitment, the programmes are hard to find on a The University and College Admissions Service (UCAS) search as they are listed as 'Business Management – Other'. To find a course with enterprise and/or entrepreneurship in the title, a prospective student would have to actively look for one using these specific terms. Many students do not know that such programmes exist and find them by chance.
- In some instances, students feel that the balance between theory (about entrepreneurship) and application (for entrepreneurship) is wrong. Some believe that there is too much theory, others too much practice. In reality, it is hard to find this balance for all students. The larger the group, the greater the variability in expectation on the balance between theory and practice.

- Linked with these is the students' perception of themselves as 'entrepreneurs'. Some students get dispirited if they have not got a 'viable' idea by the time they are approaching year 2. This is exacerbated if they see other students progressing faster than they are.
- The assessment strategy is partly built around them having a business idea to work on. Students who cannot settle on an idea struggle with some aspects of the assignments. Various approaches have been tried to circumvent this problem, such as giving students businesses to work on and various forms of collaboration. None is quite as effective as a student's own business idea.
- While attrition is accepted on all programmes, with low initial numbers the loss of students becomes quite pronounced.
- Institutionally the programmes become highly visible and as such is often challenged to produce a high number of successful start-ups. The nature of the programmes, in this respect, is not well understood.

The BA EE, in its current iteration, aims to strike a balance between modules that focus on entrepreneurship in practice and those that aim to develop a deeper understanding of the theory of business management and entrepreneurship. The third dimension to the programme is personal entrepreneurial development (PED). The strong PED focus was intended to be the entirely bespoke element of the programme, designed to support students' development at a pace relevant to their needs. The BA EE structure is outlined in Fig. 3.2.

Experience of running the course and the changing nature of the cohorts has again resulted in a reappraisal of the programme. Perhaps the enduring nature of enterprise and entrepreneurship programmes is the need to constantly evolve them.

MA in Global Entrepreneurship

MA GE was introduced in 2009 to provide a progression pathway for BA students wishing to continue their studies and also to provide a programme of study for people from other disciplines who wished to explore a business idea in a global context. The programme is flexible enough to be able to accommodate mature people, with considerable experience, wishing to develop a new business venture or wishing to expand an existing business into a new market.

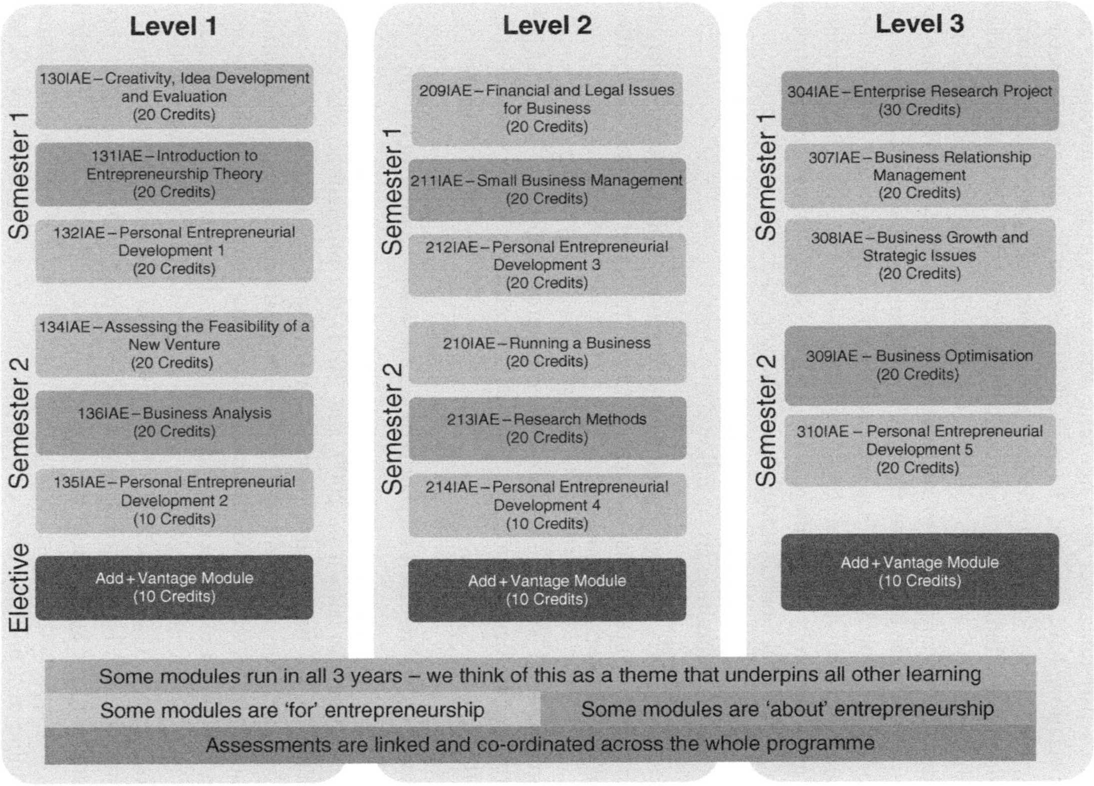

3 COVENTRY UNIVERSITY

Level 1 — Semester 1
- 130IAE – Creativity, Idea Development and Evaluation (20 Credits)
- 131IAE – Introduction to Entrepreneurship Theory (20 Credits)
- 132IAE – Personal Entrepreneurial Development 1 (20 Credits)

Level 1 — Semester 2
- 134IAE – Assessing the Feasibility of a New Venture (20 Credits)
- 136IAE – Business Analysis (20 Credits)
- 135IAE – Personal Entrepreneurial Development 2 (10 Credits)

Level 1 — Elective
- Add+Vantage Module (10 Credits)

Level 2 — Semester 1
- 209IAE – Financial and Legal Issues for Business (20 Credits)
- 211IAE – Small Business Management (20 Credits)
- 212IAE – Personal Entrepreneurial Development 3 (20 Credits)

Level 2 — Semester 2
- 210IAE – Running a Business (20 Credits)
- 213IAE – Research Methods (20 Credits)
- 214IAE – Personal Entrepreneurial Development 4 (10 Credits)
- Add+Vantage Module (10 Credits)

Level 3 — Semester 1
- 304IAE – Enterprise Research Project (30 Credits)
- 307IAE – Business Relationship Management (20 Credits)
- 308IAE – Business Growth and Strategic Issues (20 Credits)

Level 3 — Semester 2
- 309IAE – Business Optimisation (20 Credits)
- 310IAE – Personal Entrepreneurial Development 5 (20 Credits)
- Add+Vantage Module (10 Credits)

Some modules run in all 3 years – we think of this as a theme that underpins all other learning

Some modules are 'for' entrepreneurship   Some modules are 'about' entrepreneurship

Assessments are linked and co-ordinated across the whole programme

Fig. 3.2 BA EE structure

The course offers a balance between academic theory and practical application. It has always been taught on a block delivery basis, but has migrated from a part-time offer to a full-time offer as students' requirements and expectations have changed. Each module starts with a three-day emersion into the subject, followed by a series of four hour weekly workshops, with the assignment submitted approximately every six weeks. This model worked well for the IAE and is still used by ICTE as it helps to utilise staff teaching time more effectively. It also seems to work well for students as even those in employment can block book the time away from work to attend the three day workshops. The MA GE has increasingly attracted international students, many from a family business background. While the intention is to continue to grow the programme, there is also an interest in running the programme in international markets under a franchised or validation arrangement.

The MA GE modules are as follows:

Certificate level: creating a personal entrepreneurial framework; leadership and managing in an entrepreneurial way; opportunity recognition, exploration and exploitation; innovation

Diploma level: strategic entrepreneurship; profitability and financial performance; human resource development in a global context; marketing for entrepreneurs

Master's level: research methodology; entrepreneurship dissertation

Between the launch in 2009 and 2011, the programme was offered mainly to UK-based participants on a part-time basis. In part, this was based on the assumption that it would attract more people in employment than graduates wishing to continue their studies. The university at this time did not have a recruitment target for the IAE. Because the IAE was not a school or a faculty, no consideration was given to finding students for its programmes. The IAE was still part of CUE at this time. Ongoing discussions with the International Recruitment Office (IRO) brought the programme to the attention of the overseas agents, and from 2012 onwards it became apparent that there was greater market potential for this programme running as a full-time offer to a largely international student base. While momentum was growing through 2012/2013, changes in the IRO team resulted in the programme once again dropping off the radar.

MA in Enterprise and Entrepreneurship Education

The programme was first validated in 2008 as a top-up award to the National Centre for Entrepreneurship in Education (NCEE) International Enterprise Educators Programme (IEEP). Several attempts were made at that time to accredit a full master's programme based on the IEEP, but this was not successful for several reasons. When the programme was devised, it was conceived that the material would be delivered in a fluid, dynamic and evolving way, based on the accomplishment of a series of masteries gained over the whole programme. This approach did not lend itself easily to the more structured approach demanded by the validation process, which tends to peg specific learning outcome to individual modules.

In recent years, attitudes have shifted in favour of programmes that are less formulaic in structure and are more accommodating of portfolio assignments that recognise the interconnectedness of knowledge and which allow for a more flexible approach to teaching and assessment. This has enabled the IEEP to be accredited as the Certificate and Diploma stages of the MA EEE top-up which CU already offered.

MA EEE has been designed to meet a clearly identified need arising from the phenomenal growth of activity in the field of enterprise and entrepreneurship education in the further education and university sectors. Enterprise and entrepreneurship are still relatively new for academia. MA EEE aims to help those responsible for the design and/or delivery of enterprise support and entrepreneurship education to develop a clear and coherent strategy to underpin their provision. This will mean different things to different people and needs to be institutionally specific. The programme aims to stimulate the development of an institutional environment for enterprise and entrepreneurship by helping staff to build the resource base needed to support activity in an evolving policy context. This creates challenges for educators both conceptually and professionally in their ever-changing role. For many it demands new ways of thinking and new ways of learning.

For ICTE, enterprise and entrepreneurship education combined represent one of three pillars that underpin its approach, the others being innovation and leadership. The contextualising of education is fundamental, especially as much of its strategy is directed at transformation in an international context.

"*Governmental departments in many countries are convinced that it is possible to motivate students at tertiary institutions of education to become entrepreneurs and to start their own businesses*" (Weber 2011: 1). However, a

Table 3.3 The MA EEE structure

M100ICTE	Entrepreneurial educational challenges	PG Certificate in Enterprise and Entrepreneurship Education
M101ICTE	The entrepreneurial mindset	
M102ICTE	Entrepreneurial behaviours, skills and attributes	
M103ICTE	Opportunity recognition and new venture development	PG Diploma in Enterprise and Entrepreneurship Education
M104ICTE	Designing entrepreneurial organisations	
M105ICTE	Developing entrepreneurship education strategies	
M109IAE	Dissertation	MA in Enterprise and Entrepreneurship Education

key consideration is where this motivation will come from. The WEF argues that it must come from educational institutions and at all the levels. Institutionalising entrepreneurship within the education system is seen as a vital part of the economic future (EC 2014; Young 2014). What this call to action illustrates is that if realised, it would require an army of effective entrepreneurship educators to meet the need created. Where will these entrepreneurship educators come from?

Building on the firm foundations of the IEEP, the overall aim of this master's programme is to equip educators with a mastery of the key elements of facilitating, teaching and organising entrepreneurial learning and education across different contexts. It aims to help participants to take a leadership role in meeting these demands and also to build the capacity of further and higher education institutions. The first cohort of MA EEE will be in September 2017 (Table 3.3).

3.5 International Centre for Transformational Entrepreneurship

The IAE had survived for a long period of time, perhaps longer than it should have, because institutionally something was needed to fill a gap. In many ways, the university was unsure of what it needed the IAE to do or be and so it was asked to do everything: support students' start-up, generate revenue, be a commercial centre and an academic centre. It needed to produce world-class research outputs and establish itself as a brand of excellence in enterprise and entrepreneurship both internally and externally. On 1 August 2015, the IAE was restructured and closed down and all educational programmes were moved over to ICTE.

The creation of ICTE is a mark of institutional maturity with respect to its role in entrepreneurship and enterprise thinking and their role in social change. ICTE feel that a need exists for renewed thinking on how enterprise and entrepreneurship can support socio-economic growth in the local, regional, national and international environment. Current challenges within this environment indicate that novel approaches are required to address them and to find sustainable solutions. A dedicated focus is needed to spearhead transformational entrepreneurship. This dedicated focus will be provided by ICTE, and its aim is now to make a substantial contribution to entrepreneurship education, entrepreneurial leadership, innovation, socio-economic development and policy formulation. By placing ICTE wholly in the academic sphere, it has created a space, for the first time, for entrepreneurship to flourish at CU. In line with the university's research strategy, ICTE has replaced its commercial arm with a research focus which supports a more consistent and clear focus.

3.6 Lessons Learnt

Various lessons were learnt from the IAE and ICTE, namely:

- There is a belief that to be effective, enterprise centres, specifically those with a strong entrepreneurship education focus, should sit outside business schools. This case study would on balance agree with this approach. However, it might also caution that isolation brings additional stresses that could be avoided if a more substantial infrastructure had been provided.
- Building on the above, the IAE's revenue structure was critically dependent upon its teaching activities. However, not being in a faculty meant that it was not given access to the very resources it needed to effectively recruit. Working on 'both sides of the ring road' meant that it was answerable to two 'masters'. Being part of CUE, the IAE was expected to generate surplus revenue as a commercial subsidiary, yet it did not seem to have access to the CU services that were vital to its survival as an academic unit. It nevertheless was required to make a substantial contribution to CU revenue (directly and via its CUE surplus).

- From the perspective of students, the IAE was part of the business school anyway, they saw no difference. From the perspective of academic staff, the IAE staff were in a sense academic outsiders and to some not really academics at all. As a faculty home, the business school had the power to accept or reject programme or module changes and had oversight of all academic data and finances. While the IAE may have 'basked in the glory of the occasional spotlight', such as Entrepreneurial University of the Year (2011), it faced many struggles to establish its true value in the institution overall.
- The creation of ICTE presented an opportunity to stop and appraise what the role of such a centre might be. It has long been the desire of the IAE to change. The change that resulted was the positioning of the new centre within the ring road (CU) and to effectively sever its role as a commercial subsidiary. The decision was made to allow ICTE to focus on teaching and researching, and it was given the opportunity and the challenge to become the centre of excellence it was always expected to be.

3.7 Conclusion

Whilst the aforementioned text might suggest that the IAE did not achieve its goals and ambitions, it did achieve a great deal. The question that this case study raises most is where centres such as this should be positioned within the HEI. The creation of a robust and independent centre requires a great deal of institutional support, both financial and ideological. ICTE has this now.

References

EC (2014). Thematic Working Group on entrepreneurship education, Final report, Brussels, November. Available at http://ec.europa.eu/education/policy/strategic-framework/archive/documents/entrepreneurship-report-2014_en.pdf

Finkle, T. A., Kuratko, D. F., & Goldsby, M. G. (2006). An examination of entrepreneurship centres in the United States: A National Survey. *Journal of Small Business Management, 44*(2), 184–206.

Finkle, T. A., Menzies, T. V., Kuratko, D. F., & Goldsby, M. G. (2012). Financial Activities of entrepreneurship centres in the United States. *Journal of Business and Entrepreneurship, 23*(2), 48–64.

Kretz, A., & Creso, S. (2013). Third stream, fourth mission: Perspectives on university engagement with economic relevance. *Higher Education Policy, 26*, 497-5-6.

Lackeus, (2013). Developing entrepreneurial competencies: An action-based approach and classification in education, Thesis for the Degree of Licentiate of Engineering, Chalmers University of Technology, Göteborg.

Lockyer, J., & Adams, N. (2014). Venture creation programmes: Causation or effectuation? Ninth European Conference on Innovation and Entrepreneurship, University of Ulster, 18th to 19th September, 2014, Conference proceedings, Coleraine, pp. 287–295.

Morris, M. H., Kuratko, D. F., Schindehutte, M., & Spivack, A. J. (2011). Framing the entrepreneurial experience. *Entrepreneurship Theory and Practice*, 36(1), 11–40.

Sarasvathy, S. D. (2001a). Causation and effectuation: Toward a theoretical shift from economic inevitability to entrepreneurial contingency. *Academy of Management Review*, 26(2), 243–263.

Sarasvathy, S. D. (2001b). What makes entrepreneurs entrepreneurial? For submission to: *Harvard Business Review* (No publication data available).

Schindehutte, M., Morris, M., & Alan, J. (2006). Beyond achievement: Entrepreneurship as extreme experience. *Small Business Economics*, 27, 349–368.

Shattock, M. (ed.) (2009). *Entrepreneurialism in universities and the knowledge economy: Diversification and organisational change in European higher education.* The Society for Research into Higher Education and the Open University Press. Maidenhead: McGraw-Hill Education.

The Guardian (2015). *University League Tables.* Available at https://www.the guardian.com/education/ng-interactive/2014/jun/02/university-league-tables-2015-the-complete-list. Last accessed 14th November 2016.

Thomas, K. (2014, 8th October). The Guardian, Higher Education Network Blog. Available at https://www.theguardian.com/higher-education-net work/blog/2014/oct/08/john-latham-i-dont-want-more-studentsbut-im-glad-the-caps-going.

Weber, R. (2011). *Evaluating entrepreneurship education.* Wiesbaden: Springer DE.

World Economic Forum (2009). Educating the Next Wave of Entrepreneurs. Available at http://www3.weforum.org/docs/WEF_GEI_EducatingNextEntrepreneurs_ExecutiveSummary_2009.pdf

Young, L. (2014). The relevance of enterprise education. Department of Business Innovation and Skills (June). Available at https://www.gov.uk/government/uploads/system/uploads/attachment_data/file/338749/EnterpriseforAll-lowres-200614.pdf

Joan Lockyer is the Assistant Director, International Centre for Transformational Entrepreneurship (ICTE), at CU with main responsibility for the development and delivery of its academic programmes. Joan has worked in Higher Education for fifteen years, prior to which she worked in industry for over ten years and consultancy for twelve years. Her teaching experience covers the full spectrum of accredited and non-accredited programme. She is an experienced enterprise educator, leading on the development of the Master's in Enterprise and Entrepreneurship Education. She has developed a range of modules that support enterprise and entrepreneurship skills development in undergraduates, regardless of discipline. She has successfully delivered/contributed to a number of European projects, with a total value of over five million euros. Her research interests embrace entrepreneurship in a range of contexts, but with a focus on the transformative effect of entrepreneurship through education, leadership and innovation.

CHAPTER 4

Lancaster University

Fionnuala Schultz, Helen Fogg, Eleanor Hamilton and Sarah Jack

Abstract This case study illustrates how the Institute for Entrepreneurship and Enterprise Development was transformed into the Department for Entrepreneurship, Strategy and Innovation (DESI). Since its inception, the focus has been on three key elements – research, education and business support. Through externally funded projects, DESI has assisted more than 2,500 SMEs during the last ten years, resulting in significant performance improvements and business growth in the small- and medium-sized enterprises supported. DESI sees its ability to combine top-class research rigour and impactful business engagement as being critical to their strategy and its ability to inspire, build, develop and support current and future leaders of a wide range of organisations. Over the next few years, DESI will further develop its reputation as a global leader in entrepreneurship and strategy research; enhance its teaching programmes at the undergraduate, postgraduate and executive education levels in a way that reflects its united identity and capitalises on its distinctive assets; and build a sustainable portfolio of business engagement projects capable of making substantial impacts at many levels.

F. Schultz (✉) · H. Fogg · E. Hamilton · S. Jack
Lancaster University, Lancaster, UK
e-mail: f.schultz@lancaster.ac.uk; h.fogg@lancaster.ac.uk; e.hamilton@lancaster.ac.uk; s.l.jack@lancaster.ac.uk

© The Author(s) 2017
G. Maas, P. Jones (eds.), *Entrepreneurship Centres*,
DOI 10.1007/978-3-319-47892-0_4

Keywords Research · Education · Business support · Innovation · SMEs

4.1 INTRODUCTION

Established in 2002, the Institute for Entrepreneurship and Enterprise Development (IEED) (until 2015), now the Department for Entrepreneurship, Strategy and Innovation (DESI), recognised the growing prominence of the academic study of entrepreneurship. Since its inception, the focus has been on three key elements – research, education and business support. A unique academic department within a business school, DESI offers a comprehensive suite of support to small- and medium-sized enterprises (SMEs) which is constantly developed to meet the changing demands of the sector. Its approach has been informed by fifteen years of world-class research and engagement with entrepreneurs. This has led to a sophisticated and informed understanding of SME engagement and learning processes. Through projects part-financed by the European Union (EU), Northwest Regional Development Agency and Higher Education Innovation Fund, DESI has assisted more than 2,500 SMEs during the last ten years, resulting in significant performance improvements and business growth in the SMEs supported.

4.2 BACKGROUND OF LANCASTER UNIVERSITY

Lancaster University was founded in 1964. The founding subjects were in natural sciences, business subjects and humanities, while the second generation of subjects focused on social sciences and technology. Lancaster University is highly ranked in each of the UK's major university league tables, including the *Guardian* (10th), the *Complete University Guide* (9th) and the *Times* (11th). The University has an outstanding research reputation and continuously seeks to identify ways in which its research can be applied for the good of society. This includes the development of three knowledge business centres: InfoLab21, the Management School and the Lancaster Environment Centre. Today Lancaster University has four faculties: Arts and Social Sciences, Health and Medicine, Science and Technology and Lancaster University Management School (LUMS). LUMS was the first faculty to be established. The University has about 12,000 full-time students and approximately 700 academic staff, out of a total staff complement of over 2,000. Lancaster University is one of the leading UK academic institutions in terms of the volume and scope of its partnerships with SMEs (Higher Education Business and Community Interaction survey 2008/2009). It has delivered over 50 projects supported through EU, national and regional funds with a combined total value in excess of £100 million since 2001; working with over 5,000 companies since 1999. These projects have led to the creation of over 250 new businesses and 4,300 new jobs in SMEs. Projects engage in a wide range of business types, including leadership development, management innovation, eco innovation, information and communications technologies, advanced manufacturing, design and enterprise. For fifteen years, Lancaster University has embraced business engagement as a strategic priority. The University has a dedicated central department which oversees contracting, financial reporting and quality. Faculties have dedicated staff who engage with businesses in various ways to ensure that the full range of research and innovation across the University's research community is accessible. Our award-winning facilities for businesses in the Environment Centre and InfoLab21 are the best of their kind; office spaces were highlighted as an exemplar in a government report on university–business interactions (https://www.gov.uk/government/uploads/system/uploads/).

Lancaster University has expertise in delivery of multiple partner projects. Examples include the European Regional Development Fund (ERDF) part-financed Centre for Global Eco-Innovation, which unites the expertise, resources and global contacts of Lancaster University, the University of Liverpool and the international commercialisation consultancy of Inventya Ltd. Other projects delivered by DESI will be further discussed in Section 4.8 of this case study.

At the national level, evidence for Lancaster's standing is abundant. Lancaster's research and activities with SMEs have received several rounds of competitive funding from the Economic and Social Research Council (ESRC). LUMS was also awarded £32 million from the Regional Growth Fund (RGF) for the Wave 2 Growth Hubs (W2GH) programme, overseeing and managing funds disbursed across 16 English city regions. Collectively, these RGF projects will benefit thousands of businesses, and it is expected that more than 4,000 jobs will have been created through this programme by 2017 (please see for further details http://www.lancaster.ac.uk/lums/business/business-growth/programmes/wave2/).

Internationally, Lancaster's EU-funded projects have involved numerous links in Europe through, for example, Knowledge Acceleration and Responsible Innovation Meta-network (KARIM) and the Nano Regions Alliance. The Lancaster China Catalyst Programme (LCCP) takes their work to China, providing a bridge for Lancashire businesses. Through membership of the US-based Berkeley (University) Innovation Forum (BIF), Lancaster links to a network of global leaders in open innovation, and the Lancashire Giants project recently took a group of Lancashire business owners on an innovation journey to Silicon Valley. In 2014, DESI played a leading role in LUMS achieving Gold Status in the Small Business Charter initiative. The Small Business Charter award demonstrates how Business Schools connect with a world-class network of SMEs and enterprises.

Collectively, these examples provide relevant evidence of Lancaster's standing at local, national and international levels. They illustrate how policymakers, research funders, government, independent reviewers and prize-awarding committees assess and value Lancaster's work. Most importantly, Lancaster can demonstrate a large client base of business owners and managers who provide Lancaster with repeat business and many new referrals. Lancaster sees their support for their work as the litmus test of their standing in the SME community.

4.3 Background of the Region in which the University Operates

Lancaster University is a campus university located just outside of Lancaster, a historic and vibrant city just 15 min away from campus by bus. Some details on the North West of England are shown in Table 4.1.

4.4 Background of the Centre and History of the Entrepreneurship Provision

LUMS started teaching entrepreneurship in the 1980s; the first entrepreneurship unit with teaching and researching activities was then established in 1999. In 2003, this unit became the IEED which gained departmental status in 2008. The department relaunched the Centre

Table 4.1 Data on the North West of England

Metric	North West England
Gross disposable household income (€)	18,949 (90.3 % of UK average)
Share of UK gross value added (GVA)	9.4 %
Total regional GVA (€)	160.6 billion
Employment rate	69.8 %
Manufacturing industry share of UK GVA	13.3 %
Population	7,052,177 (2011 census)
Size (km^2)	14,100
Composition of regional GVA	Service industries: 50 %
	Production industries: 28 %
	Distribution industries: 14 %
	Construction industries: 8 %
Proportion of working-age population with no qualifications	14 %
Total spending on R&D (€)	3.8 billion
Higher education institutions	12 universities
Number of students	250,000
Number of patents	2013: 1,260 applications, 183 granted
Number of firms	2012: 532,000: SMEs (0–249 employees): 532,000 Employers: 132,000

Source: Office of National Statistics (2013), Lancashire Enterprise Partnership (2014), The Migration Observatory at the University of Oxford (2013), Office for National Statistics (2012), Office of National Statistics (2011), Intellectual Property Office (2014)

for Family Business in 2014 with the appointment and involvement of internationally distinguished scholars and practitioners. The latest change has been the repositioning of the Sir Roland Smith Centre for Strategic Management within IEED in August 2015 which led to the new DESI.

DESI is well known for generating high-quality and engaged research which is funded through different sources, primarily through a range of external funding bodies. The Department has achieved high visibility in the entrepreneurship, strategy and innovation global research communities. It is increasingly recognised as an international leader for research and education in entrepreneurship and innovation, in partnership with business and the community.

DESI undertakes outstanding work in research, education and business support. Its strengths derive from the close alignment of these three key elements and from the continuous 'real world' feedback received through interaction with the business community. Founding all operations upon the real and current demands of business is fundamental to the department and has been critical to its growth. Every process, product and stage of activity within the department is informed by dialogue and engagement with businesses and external organisations. This generates a constantly expanding knowledge base which shapes the development and delivery of research, teaching and business support. This ensures that these activities are always up to date, focused and precisely matched to the needs of students, businesses and the wider community.

DESI's objectives are best reflected in their vision: "*to become the global exemplar in entrepreneurship and strategy education with a World-wide reputation for our ability to combine top-class research rigor and impactful business engagement in order to inspire, develop and support the current and future leaders of forward-looking organizations*".

DESI is part of LUMS. LUMS consists of 7 departments and 11 centres. Today, DESI consists of 21 full-time academics, 1 distinguished scholar, 2 emeritus professors, 16 honorary scholars, 12 members of staff working in business engagement and 24 PhD students.

4.5 Location within Lancaster University

Lancaster University has a long and successful track record in publicly funded projects to support SMEs. Lancaster University's strategic plan for 2020 articulates the aim of active engagement with businesses which is met by the wide range of business engagement activities within its faculties – LUMS, Faculty of Science and Technology, Faculty of Arts and Social Sciences and Faculty of Health and Medicine. The aim 'To engage actively with students, businesses and our communities' is one of the top three priorities within the University's 2020 strategy. The overall strategic commitment to be a globally significant university puts engagement at the heart of its mission. This includes engagement with new communities through expansion of its overseas presence, engagement with alumni and students, engagement with businesses (including SMEs), policymakers and other agents of social and economic change and development (including charities, non-governmental organisations and international organisations). A major part of Lancaster University's engagement also comes through its important role within its community of Lancaster and the North West of England. This approach has enabled the University to position itself as an entrepreneurial university. This has been achieved in a number of ways but especially through its ability to engage and support its communities at all levels – regional, national and international.

4.6 CURRICULUM

DESI strives to improve the student learning experience and provide transferable skills, at every level of learning and teaching, from undergraduate to PhD research. The Department encourages students to gain work-based experience though direct involvement with businesses. This activity supports the programmes run within DESI and also the service teaching it delivers across LUMS consortial programmes.

Undergraduate Studies

DESI delivers a three-year bachelor's degree in Management and Entrepreneurship plus a four-year variant of this programme which includes a one-year industry placement. Students are immersed in a network of world-class academics and Entrepreneurs-in-Residence (EiR) to help them explore what it means to be an entrepreneur. They are challenged to explore entrepreneurship in different contexts and from different world views to develop their skills and extend their knowledge. Employers want graduates who are able to act entrepreneurially, evaluate new ideas and understand the challenges of taking ideas to market. DESI has embraced this position through the programmes they design and deliver in partnership with the business community.

SMEs are often very innovative and entrepreneurial. This context is used as an important foundation for understanding how entrepreneurship comes about. This also provides an important foundation for exploring entrepreneurship within other contexts, such as large global organisations, family businesses, social enterprises and franchises. DESI ensures that the integration of theory and practice is embedded in the programme, with a network of over 50 EiR supporting our world-class researchers. Enacted, observational and situated learning styles are used, alongside traditional lectures, to help build a deeper understanding of theory and how this works in practice.

The four-year degree provides an opportunity for students to spend a year on industrial placement. During this year, the emphasis is on the practical application and evaluation of theories and concepts learnt through the programme. Students gain unique insights that underpin the final year of their studies, providing students with skills and knowledge that are valued by potential employers, in addition to providing experience for future business ventures. These business engagement activities provide invaluable opportunities, crucial to supporting what DESI is able to offer students during their studies. A new Bioscience with Entrepreneurship Bachelor programme will run from autumn 2016. Aimed at students with an interest in a range of bioscience topics, this degree also provides an opportunity to understand the challenges of entrepreneurship and innovation.

Postgraduate Studies

There are two master's programmes dedicated to entrepreneurship: The MSc in Entrepreneurship, Innovation and Practice and the MSc in International Innovation (Entrepreneurship). DESI also runs two further master's programmes which focus on strategy. The MSc in Entrepreneurship, Innovation and Practice is a one-year master's programme which includes building understanding about entrepreneurship and how it works in practice, corporate entrepreneurship, family enterprise, innovation in practice, new venture creation and strategic management. With a strong focus on the practical application of theory, this master's programme equips business and non-business graduates with the knowledge and skills to be innovative and enterprising in their future careers. The programme emphasises theoretical rigour and practical learning, benefitting from the academic excellence and broad business networks provided by DESI with several modules drawing upon its EiR network. The programme is designed for students who want to start their own business, work as an 'intrapreneur' and/or be an innovator in an existing company, take over a family business or work in entrepreneurship and innovation-related fields (e.g. consulting, public support programmers).

The MSc in International Innovation (Entrepreneurship) is a unique programme which offers a groundbreaking curriculum, blending academic studies, company projects with UK and Chinese businesses and cultural experiences. Students receive a tax-free bursary (tuition fees still apply) and can join one of six specialist pathways, including entrepreneurship. Through the entrepreneurship pathway, students gain in-depth understanding about entrepreneurship but also study design, technology and Chinese language and culture (or equivalent for Chinese speakers). Two collaborative projects with industry are undertaken; one with a UK business and one with a China-based business. Entrepreneurship studies include corporate entrepreneurship, design-driven innovation, family enterprise management, innovation in practice and new venture creation.

The European Masters in Management is delivered in partnership with EMLYON Business School and Ludwig Maximilian University of Munich. This Masters is co-designed around the MSc in Management and the MSc in Entrepreneurship Innovation and Practice. It is a two-year general management master programme based in France, Germany and the UK.

The International Business and Strategy MSc combines the global perspective of international business with up-to-date strategic thinking required to develop competitive advantage and implement effective organisational designs. Overall, the programme provides students with a strong interdisciplinary grounding in all aspects of international business and strategy.

PhD Programme

Within the department, there is also a vibrant PhD community with currently 24 PhD students. These PhD students are an integral part of the departmental research community. PhD students are invited to engage with the activities of the Department and given the space and support to develop their research and academic interests. PhD students are also invited to contribute to research programmes within the Department. The access to experienced staff and resources in the University are essential to the success of the PhD students and is provided by DESI.

4.7 Research

Research activities within DESI focus around three main themes:

- Entrepreneurship, with a particular focus upon entrepreneurial learning, family business, enterprise policy and regional development, networks and SMEs.

- Strategy, in which a strategy-as-practice perspective foregrounds the work of strategy actors, strategy process and micro-level aspects of strategy in various contexts.
- Innovation, including social process and social practice.

DESI is one of the leading centres for research in entrepreneurship, ranked no. 7 in the world by a recent Elsevier publications and citations analysis, and ranked 2nd in the UK, after London Business School. DESI differentiates itself through incorporation of a strong and active business engagement group that offers a distinctive link to practice. DESI is also home to the Centre for Family Business and a leading research group in strategic management (formerly known as the Sir Roland Smith Centre for Strategic Management). In September 2015, *Family Capital*, an influential practice-oriented journal, listed LUMS among the top 25 in the world for family business. Strategy-as-Practice forms a unifying theme for the research group in strategic management. It encompasses both the formulation of strategy and how strategies are put into action to deliver strategic renewal and change. The co-location of the different research interests and the business engagement activities offers opportunities for high-quality research which supports, and is supported by, research-led business engagement ensuring an impactful and distinctive research profile strongly linked to practice.

4.8 Engagement Activity/Programmes for SME

Lancaster University's engagement with SMEs is long-standing and offers a comprehensive ecosystem of support for entrepreneurs and new enterprises from initial idea to successful business across all faculties. Lancaster's engagement and development of SMEs is a strategic priority. As such, Lancaster's regional, national and international engagement with SMEs is wide-ranging and has attracted extensive funding. In 2013, DESI won an inaugural national award from ESRC for its outstanding impact in business.

What these illustrate is that DESI's business engagement strategy is critical to the growth of the Department but also integral to its research and teaching strategies. Through successful integration it is informed by research but also used to inform research. It is an approach which has enabled DESI to maximise opportunities to expand and diversify income, including research income. It also delivers impact, enhances student recruitment, experience and employability, and contributes to policy and practice.

Entrepreneurs-in-Residence

In 2008, DESI decided to host within the department an EiR – Ian Gordon. Over the following two years he worked with DESI on its internal approach to business and the range of programmes to support entrepreneurs. Ian was tasked to act as a 'cultural irritant', challenging assumptions and informing SME programme delivery. The result has been a step change in DESI's provision and the overhaul of some of the business support programmes. The success of DESI's founding EiR allowed DESI to expand this initiative which, since its conception in 2008, has seen the number of EIRs working with DESI increase to 29 in 2012 and 54 in the spring of 2016. DESI aims to continue to grow this number and also invite key international stakeholders to join DESI's EiR programme. While this increase really pushes forward the diverse set of business support programmes DESI offers, more critically it builds diversity, depth and breadth into departmental research but also teaching, and the experiences students are exposed to.

All of DESI's entrepreneurs are long-standing associates of the University and are active across teaching and business engagement, making contributions as ambassadors and advocates diverse. This form of activity demonstrates DESI's sustained effort to engage practitioners in the co-design and delivery of business support. Lancaster University's experience is summarised in 'What is (the point of) an entrepreneur-in-residence?'.

Lancashire and Cumbria Regional Growth programmes for SMEs

These programmes are designed to give SME owner-managers tools to grow their business through working with a world-class University. Each programme involves the establishment of a 'forum' which is a facilitated network for a select group of successful and aspirational SMEs to come together and cross-fertilise ideas and opportunities and further be directed towards wider Lancaster University business engagement programmes across the faculties. The Lancashire Forum is part of Boost Business Lancashire, the Lancashire's Business Growth Hub. This programme is a peer network and business masterclass programme designed for SME owner-managers. The Forum, designed to inspire and foster a culture which supports and brings together ambitious growth businesses, supports 80 SMEs. This model has been extremely successful and DESI has now commenced a similar programme in Cumbria, with plans to expand delivery throughout the North West of England and beyond.

The Innovation, Design, Entrepreneurship and Science at Daresbury Project

The Innovation, Design, Entrepreneurship and Science (IDEAS) at Daresbury project worked with 60 'technology focused' SMEs to explore how they could be supported to facilitate growth. Workshops conducted at Daresbury Science and Innovation Campus resulted in 55 jobs being created and 10 safeguarded. The programme provided business owners with an understanding of their networks, based on research indicating that business growth can be stimulated by optimising the variety of contacts available to them. The programme focused on customer-focused innovation, competitive advantages through people and processes and beyond networking: creativity, collaboration and growth. The IDEAS at Daresbury project was shortlisted for the Praxis Unico Impact Awards.

Regional Growth Fund – Wave 2 Growth Hub (W2GH) Programme

Lancaster University has a strong track record in the project management of large-scale, multipartnership outreach programmes, and based on this was awarded an unprecedented role for a university, implementing governmental policy through the design, delivery and evaluation of a £32 million RGF W2GH programme. The W2GH programme was an 18-month initiative, led by LUMS. The programme started in 2013 and was finished in 2015.

A network of 15 'Growth Hubs' were created in partnership with local councils, local enterprise partnerships (LEPs), universities and chambers of commerce. The extent of the W2GH community included 17 LEPs, 42 universities, 19 chambers of commerce and over 200 local and national business representative, support and innovation organisations, alongside the Department for Business Innovation and Skills, the Cabinet Office and the Department for Communities and Local Government. The Growth Hubs played a strategic role in signposting and coordinating national and local business support, offering targeted support tailored to the needs of entrepreneurs in the context of their local economy. Each of the Hubs has its own characteristics with varying support packages tailored to the characteristics of their local industries and markets. This knowledge exchange was facilitated through a programme of events on key issues across the network, for example, evaluation, stakeholder analysis and workshops on business support in manufacturing and trade. The team at Lancaster University supported the Hubs through regular visits, attendance at key strategic meetings, promotion and sharing of activities on social media, through video testimonials and SME case studies.

As of December 2015, 3,201 new jobs have been created. By the conclusion of the monitoring period, March 2017, the hubs predict that a total of 4,160 jobs will be created, far exceeding the initial target. The programme has attracted over £66 million of private sector investment from SMEs to match the initial input of £30 million by the hubs. Thus, the programme exceeded the target of £2 private sector investment for every £1 invested. By December 2015, it was estimated that over 67,000 SMEs had engaged with their local Growth Hubs. Due to the success of the programme, LUMS was invited to a House of Commons Committee to inform policy on Government Support for Business. The W2GH programme was one of 30 innovations selected at the Deans Conference of the AACSB International, in Florida, USA, in February 2016 (the global accrediting body and membership association for business schools) for the Association's 'Innovations That Inspire' initiative. In 2015, the programme won the prestigious 'Impact Runner-Up Award' by the Academy of Management Practice Theme Committee Research Centre in recognition of the outstanding contribution and impact on society and the economy. Figure 4.1 summarises the research output generated through the W2GH programme.

LEAD

LEAD, a 10-month intensive leadership and management development programme for owner-managers, MDs and senior managers of SMEs, was derived from research into entrepreneurial learning. LEAD's integrated learning model addresses varied learning styles. These include an overnight experiential, coaching, masterclasses, action learning sets, shadowing and exchanges, and a LEAD forum. It provides a framework for the leader to innovate and grow their business through increased profitability, productivity and employment. LEAD helps develop a more strategic approach to business, using elements designed to challenge participants' thinking and ways of working. LEAD was first developed in 2003;

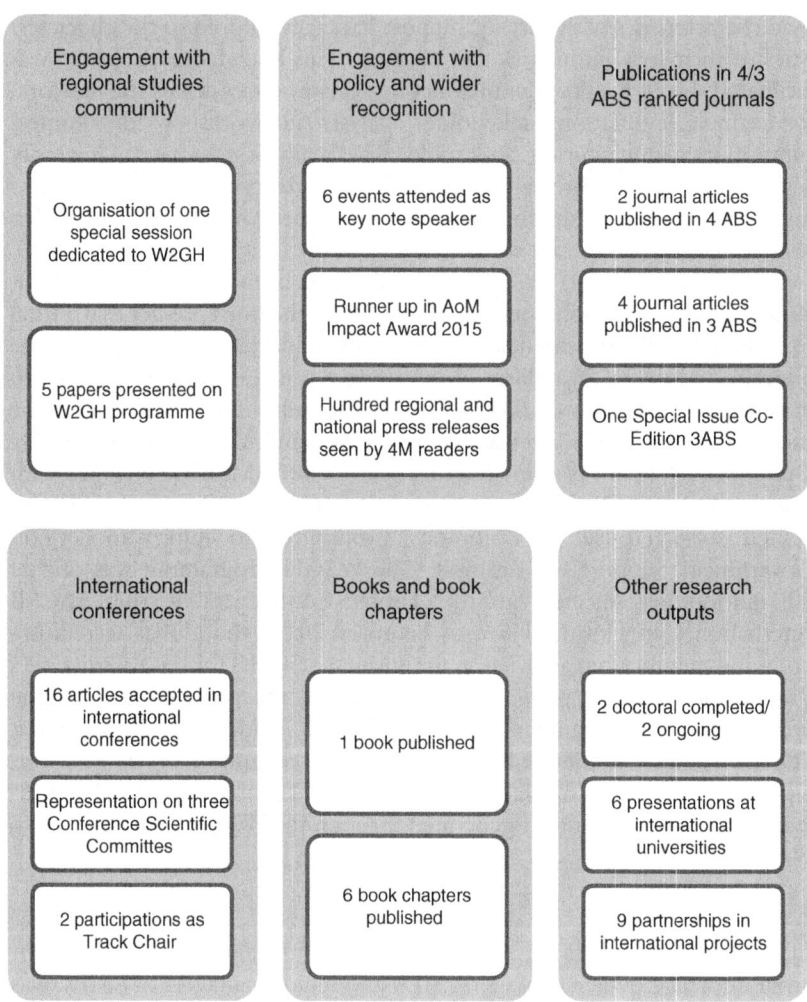

Fig. 4.1 Overall research outputs within the W2GH programme until June 2015

participants cover all sectors and demonstrate strong growth orientation. The LEAD programme has grown from provision within one English region to a model increasingly and widely promoted by other providers nationally. LEAD has been reviewed and revised, based on learning from its widespread delivery, and has been relaunched as LEAD 2 Innovate in 2014. This programme leverages LEAD principles towards innovation outcomes. It also recognises the particular challenges SME ownermanagers are facing by trying to innovate successfully while at the same time maintaining core businesses. Participants make a significant contribution to the cost of this programme via fees.

LEAD alumni exceed 1,700 companies, employ an estimated 30,000 people and turn over an estimated £1 billion – equivalent to a major corporation. In an independent evaluation (Wren and Jones 2012), participants reported post-LEAD mean annual turnover growth rates of 13.8 % and employment growth of 16.8 %, with 70 % reporting profit increase and 65 % reporting productivity increase. LEAD companies employ an additional 3,315 staff each year. LEAD has informed policy initiatives (MacLeod and Clarke 2009) and has also been identified in a House of Lords report as exemplary (http://www.publications.parliament.uk/pa/ld201213/ldselect/ldsmall/131/13102.htm).

London Creative and Digital Fusion Project

LUMS led a £5.8 million programme, part financed by ERDF, to support growth in creative and digital SMEs in London, between 2012 and 2014. Through its London base at the Work Foundation, LUMS and Imagination Lancaster partnered with Queen Mary University of London, the Centre for Creative Collaboration (University of London), Council for Industry and Higher Education and the Royal College of Art to deliver this programme for the Greater London Authority (GLA). Specific activities included

- Fuse phase (Interactive workshops): over 150 workshop and masterclass events and over 10,000 h of business support delivered
- Create phase (supported collaborations): over 10,000 h of business support
- An evaluation of the programme took place in November 2014: 68 % of respondents reported development of new skills; 67 % have a clear idea of the steps needed to achieve goals, 63 % increased confidence, 57 % new collaborations and 52 % increased ambition

Through a programme of interactive, tailored support aimed to drive sustainable innovation and growth into London's creative and digital

SMEs, the project concluded in December 2014, having supported 526 SMEs and created 246 jobs. A strong relationship was developed with the Work Foundation, GLA and a number of institutions within London upon which future activity can be developed.

International Collaborations: Berkeley Innovation Forum

The BIF is an exclusive membership group consisting of carefully selected corporate directors deeply engaged in managing innovation within their company. LUMS was invited to join BIF in 2012. Lancaster remains the only university in a unique global network of Fortune 100 companies, led by Henry Chesbrough. This has informed the development of programmes that link small and large organisations, both public and private.

International Collaborations: KARIM

The KARIM project was designed to help SMEs in north west Europe access innovation support and technology and make the region more competitive by creating a network of centres collaborating on technology transfer. The KARIM project was structured into 17 actions which brought together a partnership of eight organisations, including innovation support agencies, universities, regional government agencies and SME support organisations.

International collaborations: Lancaster China Catalyst Programme

The LCCP (please see for further details http://www.lancaster.ac.uk/news/articles/2013/lancaster-university-toexploit-its-global-reach-for-the- benefit-of-uk-smes/) is a £5.1 million development aiming to revitalise the UK's position in global export markets, create 240 jobs, help 400 domestic businesses and boost the economy by £40 million. It supports the development of a significant number of partnerships between UK SMEs and Chinese companies. Business partnerships focus on the research, development and commercialisation of new products and services for major export markets. With funding from the Higher Education Funding Council for England (£3.5 million), Lancashire County Council (£0.5 million) and Guangdong Provincial Office for Science and Technology, key external partners include the Chinese Academy of

Sciences, UK Trade and Investment, China-Britain Business Council and the Technology Strategy Board. The LCCP will help SMEs gain networks within China's Guangdong Province through the University's link with the Guangdong Provincial Office of Science and Technology.

4.9 Conclusion

DESI continues to strive to fulfil its vision of becoming the global leader and exemplar for entrepreneurship and strategy research and education. It sees its ability to combine top-class research rigour and impactful business engagement as being critical to this strategy and its ability to inspire, build, develop and support current and future leaders of a wide range of organisations. Over the next few years, DESI will work to achieve the following strategic goals: to further develop its reputation as a global leader in entrepreneurship and strategy research; to enhance its teaching programmes at the undergraduate, postgraduate and executive education levels in a way that reflects its united identity and capitalises on its distinctive assets; and to build a sustainable portfolio of business engagement projects capable of making substantial impacts at many levels and which attract the attention of a wide range of stakeholders, nationally and internationally.

References

Higher Education Business and Community Interaction survey 2008/2009. http://www.lancaster.ac.uk/lums/business/business-growth/programmes/wave2/http://www.publications.parliament.uk/pa/ld201213/ldselect/ldsmall/131/13102.htm.https://www.gov.uk/government/uploads/system/uploads/

Intellectual Property Office (2014). Facts and figures 2013/2014 calendar years. https://www.gov.uk/government/uploads/system/uploads/attachment_data/file/456097/Facts_and_Figures_2015.pdf

Lancashire Enterprise Partnership (2014). Lancashire Strategic Economic Plan, a Growth Deal for the Arc of Prosperity. https://www.lepnetwork.net/modules/downloads/download.php?file_name=22

MacLeod, D., & Clarke, N. (2009). Engaging for success: Enhancing performance through employee engagement. http://dera.ioe.ac.uk/1810/1/file52215.pdf

Office for National Statistics (2012). Summary: UK Non-Financial Business Economy, 2012 Regional Results. http://www.ons.gov.uk/businessindustryandtrade/business/businessservices/bulletins/uknonfinancialbusinesseconomyannualbusinesssurvey/2014-07-23

Office of National Statistics (2011). Regional Trends 43 2010/2011.

Office of National Statistics (2013). Regional Profile of North West – Economy. http://webarchive.nationalarchives.gov.uk/20160105160709/http://www.ons.gov.uk/ons/rel/regional-trends/region-and-country-profiles/economy--june-2013/economy—north-west–june-2013.html

The Migration Observatory at the University of Oxford (2013). North West: Census Profile. http://www.migrationobservatory.ox.ac.uk/wp-content/uploads/2016/04/CensusProfile-North_West.pdf

Wren, & Jones (2012). Quantitative Evaluation of the LEAD Programme, 2004–11, Lancaster University. https://www.lancaster.ac.uk/media/lancaster-university/content-assets/documents/lums/business/LEADeval2011.pdf

Fionnuala Schultz joined Lancaster University Management School in 2015 as a Business Consultancy Fellow. After obtaining her PhD from the University of Bremen, Fionnuala worked for Detecon (Switzerland) as a consultant in the area of performance reporting and management information systems. She has also experience of working for multinationals, working as a senior consultant in management reporting at Deutsche Telekom AG. Fionnuala is currently doing consultancy work for business support programmes.

Helen Fogg joined Lancaster University Management School in 2003 having returned from the USA where she completed an MBA at the University of Dallas, Graduate School of Management. Previously she worked for several multinational organisations including BAE Systems and the Danone Group. Helen currently leads a team developing and delivering business and management knowledge exchange programmes for industry. Her work is undertaken on a regional, national and international basis, often working collaboratively with a number of institutions.

Eleanor Hamilton served as Director of the Institute for Entrepreneurship and Enterprise Development (2002–2008), Director of Regional Affairs (2008–2016), Associate Dean for Undergraduate Studies (2009–2012) and Associate Dean for Enterprise, Engagement and Impact (2012–2015) at Lancaster University Management School. Her research interests are entrepreneurship and small business. She has worked at the interface of theory and practice and helped to secure the Chartered Association of Business School's (CABS) Small Business Charter status for Lancaster University in 2014. She recently led the Wave 2 Growth Hub programme working with 15 city regions to develop Growth Hubs across

England. In 2015–2016, Professor Hamilton co-chaired the CABS Task Force 'Business Schools: Delivering Value to Local and Regional Economies'.

Sarah Jack is Professor of Entrepreneurship at Lancaster University. Her research involves the use of qualitative methods to consider social aspects of entrepreneurship, including social networks and social capital. Her work has been published widely in international and national journals. She has received grants from various funding bodies including Knowledge Transfer Partnership, Nuffield Foundation, Carnegie Trust, ESRC and EPSRC.

CHAPTER 5

Scotland's Centres for Entrepreneurship (UK)

Robert Smith

Abstract The focus of this chapter is the collective research efficacy of Scottish Centres-for-Entrepreneurship and not upon an individual centre per se. However, the focus is not on the parochial but on the collective global reach of Scottish entrepreneurship scholars. There has been a reduction in the number and presence of active Centres and individually no one Centre has developed a critical mass. This chapter documents and evidences the entrepreneurship centre's collective efficacy and highlights lessons learnt in the process. It also identifies possible future approaches for entrepreneurship centres from the perspective of potential implications for policy and practice for higher education institutions.

Keywords Scotland · Entrepreneurship · Scottish School · Policy · Practice · HEIs

5.1 Introduction

Scotland has a proud 'Entrepreneurial Heritage' (Checkland 1976; McCrone 2001), and in the past thirty years has seen a resurgence of the 'Entrepreneurial' which is particularly evident in its Universities.

R. Smith (✉)
University of the West of Scotland, Dumfries, UK
e-mail: rob.smith@uws.ac.uk

© The Author(s) 2017
G. Maas, P. Jones (eds.), *Entrepreneurship Centres*,
DOI 10.1007/978-3-319-47892-0_5

Nevertheless, there are few studies of Entrepreneurship education in Scotland. A notable exception is the Royal Society of Edinburgh paper on Entrepreneurial Education in Scotland. This chapter reflects (autoethnographically; Muncey 2010) on the author's experience as an entrepreneurship student and scholar within the Scottish higher education institution (HEI) system. This story is as much about the author and his academic journey from mature student to Professor as it is about the future sustainability of Centres-for-Entrepreneurship. There are fifteen Scottish Universities and three other educational Institutions, and entrepreneurship is on the curriculum of most of these institutions.[1] In Scotland, entrepreneurship as an academic discipline sits within the architecture of the Business School which has had both positive and negative influences for its Centres-for-Entrepreneurship. The focus of this chapter is on the collective research efficacy of Scottish Centres-for-Entrepreneurship and not upon an individual centre per se. However, the focus is not on the parochial but on the collective global reach of Scottish entrepreneurship scholars. The research is anchored in the past, but also in the present and future. This reverie is significant given the interest of successive Scottish governments in entrepreneurship as a tool for social, cultural, economic and political growth (Making it Happen, 2015).

A major theme of this chapter is the distinctive phenomenon I refer to as the *Scottish School of Entrepreneurship* (SER). This notion builds upon earlier work (Smith 2012) and upon the author's inaugural lecture (Smith 2016). But defining exactly what constitutes SER is problematic because there are various disciplinary, historical and sociocultural elements at play in defining the meaning of the term 'Scottishness' in context. Cleary what constitutes SER is complex, subjective and a matter of interpretation just as is who is included in the category. A pragmatic decision must be made, based on origin of birth, current domicile or period of residence at a Scottish university. Moreover, the ontological development of a scholar of any nationality located at a Scottish university must be considered, as must the subject matter of their work which may have a distinctly Scottish aura to it. Thus who is a Scottish Entrepreneurship Researcher and what constitutes SER is of necessity flexible. Some scholars may not identify with the label.

The author is a product of this *Scottish School* and I am indebted to his mentors and Doctoral Supervisors – Professors Alistair R Anderson and Sarah Dodd – for their influence on his professional development. As a

PhD student at Aberdeen University in 2002, the author was fortunate to win the Raymond Family Business Award for Best Paper at the Babson-Kauffman Entrepreneurship Conference in Boulder, Colorado. This triggered a meteoric and prodigious writing career and ultimately led to him being appointed as an entrepreneurship professor. The genesis of this study began at that conference when he was introduced by Alistair to a large Scottish-based contingent of researchers including Colin Mason, Richard Harrison, David Deakins, Sarah Jack, Sarah Drakopoulou Dodd, Paul Robson, Sarah Cooper, Laura Galloway, Claire Leitch and Margaret Fletcher. This clearly demonstrated a strong Scottish 'presence' and signified an ontological sense of 'becoming, being and belongingness' which exists to this day. Some of the 'cast' are no longer Scotland based but retain links.

This apercus was also influenced by the Nordic scholar Daniel Hjorth, who conducted a study in relation to 'Nordic' Entrepreneurship Research (Hjorth 2008), and by the scholarship of Simon Down in relation to the European School of Entrepreneurship research (Down 2013). Hjorth was inspired by a perusal of the International Council for Small Business and RENT Conference participation lists which contained a disproportionably large number of Nordic scholars. Hjorth sought to identify the existence, and presence, of a Nordic School of Entrepreneurship Research as a cultural practice contributing significantly to the global entrepreneurship output. The notion of the *Scottish School* replicates his scholarship in a Scottish context. The author's aim is to more effectively understand SER. Like Hjorth, he seeks to accentuate an appreciation for the local, particular and contextual.

It is also necessary to understand SER from its recent history. To appreciate its importance and presence in the wider entrepreneurship community, it is necessary to adopt a descriptive, historical approach to story its nuances. The timeline for this research commences circa 1991. Methodologically, this allows for a more person-centred focus to emerge. Although there are a significant number of Scottish Entrepreneurship researchers, no one Centre, or Institution, has developed a critical mass. Many Centres do not have historical/archival documentation from which their story can be re-documented and reconstructed. Instead, we must consider the number of active Centres-for-Entrepreneurship, the number of internationally renowned entrepreneurship scholars and their role in stimulating and developing entrepreneurship research with a vibrant research community.

5.2 Leading from the Centres!

In the early 1990s, the Scottish government initiated a strategy for developing entrepreneurship in Scotland including a number of initiatives which shaped the nation's entrepreneurship research (Maniukiewicz et al. 1999). A seminal initiative around 1995 was the Scottish Government-sponsored Scottish Enterprise – *Local Heroes Initiative* (see Local Heroes 1997). The development of these Centres-for-Entrepreneurship helped shape entrepreneurship research in Scotland but the catalyst for change was 'The Scottish University Entrepreneurship Programme'. In 1994, Scottish Enterprise sponsored the development of existing entrepreneurship teaching within the Scottish Higher Education sector through the establishment of a number of Centres for Entrepreneurial Studies at selected institutions (see Williams and Turnbull 1997). The following Centres were initiated:

- 1994: Centre for Entrepreneurial Studies at Glasgow Caledonian University
- 1995: Centres-for-Entrepreneurship at Aberdeen University; Robert Gordon University; Napier University, Edinburgh; Stirling University; and Paisley (later UWS)
- 1996: The Strathclyde Entrepreneurship Initiative at Strathclyde University, Glasgow which later became the Hunter Centre
- 2002: Centre-for-Entrepreneurship at the University of Edinburgh

Consequently, the subsequent decades witnessed a substantial increase in the number of entrepreneurship scholars associated with Scottish Universities, an increase in the number of Centres-for-Entrepreneurship and in students undertaking entrepreneurship courses in Scottish campuses. This is testament to the collective enterprise and endeavour of individual academics, departments and universities and points to a distinctive body of SER as a potentially marketable brand. This collective endeavour engendered a growing community of interest and research practice (Lave and Wenger 1991). Another, exciting initiative between the Centres from 2007 to the present day is the Scottish Programme for Entrepreneurship which is a collaboration between Strathclyde, Edinburgh, Robert Gordon University (RGU) and Aberdeen Universities in conjunction with the Scottish Institute for Enterprise (SIE).

Collectively, the Scottish Centres-for-Entrepreneurship have impacted considerably on the landscape of enterprise education in Scotland and the UK by educating several generations and cohorts of students into an entrepreneurial mindset, many of whom would not have considered entrepreneurship and business creation as serious options prior to then. The early years were characterised by large class sizes and a missionary zeal to spread the gospel of enterprise to as many students and faculties as possible. From a pedagogical perspective, the method of delivery was the traditional lecture with an essay as the method of assessment. However, in recent years, the demand for enterprise education triggered student-led change in demand. In many Business Schools, entrepreneurship modules are offered from second-year level as compulsory. Where they are not, uptake is not as encouraging as it could be. Students want to know how to start-up a business and other practical aspects of enterprise, rather than understand entrepreneurship from a theoretical perspective. Many entrepreneurship modules are now focused on entrepreneurial processes and encouraging students to develop business ideas. Accordingly, the method of assessment has changed to trade-fayres, group work and product prototyping. Entrepreneurship theory is still taught, but the focus is more on application and practice. Interestingly, the lecturer responsible for delivering need not be an entrepreneurship specialist, which is both a strength and weakness.

However, it is in relation to research output that the collective efficacy of SER is best judged. Within the Business Schools, 'Entrepreneurship Educators' predominantly are educated to PhD level and have specialised research interests. Most of this research-active cadre are well motivated and productive albeit their research interests can be quite eclectic and difficult to manage in a programmed manner. They are often of independent mind and write and network with external scholars. Entrepreneurship scholars build their CVs upon collaborative work within the wider Entrepreneurship Research Community, thus their institutions do not benefit from their scholarly citizenship as journals editors, peer-reviewers and mentors.

The Past

It is impossible to provide a detailed history of the individual Centres in this chapter, so selected worked examples are provided. The birthplace of contemporary SER is Stirling University where in the 1990s Alistair R. Anderson, Sara Carter, Sarah Drakopoulou Dodd and Peter Rosa began their research careers. Stirling was then at the forefront of incubating entrepreneurship research and scholarship. However, the Centres created an open job market in Scotland whereby many entrepreneurship researchers migrate between Scottish universities. For example, Alistair Anderson has worked at Stirling, Aberdeen and RGU and Sara Carter at Stirling and Strathclyde. At Aberdeen University, Alistair Anderson as Deputy Director assembled a productive research team including Sarah Jack, Sarah Dodd, Mark Freel and the author before taking up his current Chair at RGU. This led to an exodus of research-active staff to RGU and a loss of critical mass at Aberdeen. Sarah Jack took over as Director before being appointed a Chair at Lancaster University. Bill Keogh in his career worked at Stirling, Aberdeen University and RGU before taking up a post of Professor at Heriot Watt before retiring. Inter-career moves are common within academia, but it is apparent that the centre of gravity within the Scottish entrepreneurship scene can change quickly. This fluidity of movement within the Scottish system is a distinctive characteristic. This ebb and flow of research-active staff is one reason many Centres do not develop critical mass.

The premier Centre in Scotland must be the Strathclyde University 'Hunter Centre'. From 2002 onwards, it has hosted the Strathclyde University entrepreneurship day which brings together active entrepreneurship researchers in Scotland to network. It now has the largest compliment of entrepreneurship researchers and Professors in Scotland – namely John Anderson, Eleanor Shaw, Jonothan Levie, Sara Carter and Sarah Drakopoulou Dodd. This production of entrepreneurship Professors and researchers of world-class status is a definite output of the initiative to set up Centres-for-Entrepreneurship. A considerable pool of talent circulates within the Scottish system. One problematic factor in writing this chapter has been to determine exactly who is a Scottish Entrepreneurship Researcher? For example, Professor Sarah Drakopoulou-Dodd is English by birth but served her academic apprenticeship at Stirling University before moving to Aberdeen University, then the RGU. She has been domiciled and worked in Greece and England. Yet, she is unmistakably part of the Scottish Entrepreneurship scene and its history. Another example is Professor Richard Harrison, an Irish scholar who has held chairs in Entrepreneurship at Aberdeen University and Edinburgh University. Similarly, Sarah Jack is now a Professor at Lancaster University but her formative years were spent at Aberdeen University. It would be possible to apply different labels to their work depending on the context in which one examined it. The work of Professor David Deakins at Paisley and his role in developing the Paisley Entrepreneurship Research Centre into a world-leading Centre and his stewardship of the Annual Rural Research

Conference are worthy of note as is the work of Professor Mike Danson at Paisley/UWs and Heriot Watt.

One of the consequences of the Scottish Government's decision to set up the Centres-of-Entrepreneurship has been the growth of Entrepreneurship research per se because the academics appointed were very active researchers and prodigious in publishing their research. They networked with each other and with colleagues nationally, internationally and globally. It is not feasible to provide a full list of scholars and discuss their achievements and outputs in detail. Instead, the author illustrates this argument by highlighting the achievements of some scholars. It is difficult to measure the tangible impact of their contribution, but in terms of the size of Scotland, it appears significant, even if only in terms of presence.

The Present

In many cases, the former Centres-of-Entrepreneurship have waned. At Stirling and Aberdeen University, there are no longer dedicated Centres due to pressures to provide a differentiated product offering in terms of teaching and research output. At UWS, this led to the inception of an *Enterprise Academy*, with its focus on Digital Enterprise and practical entrepreneurship education. With the rising pressure upon Business Schools to increase their commercialisation and income-generating activities, there is added pressure to develop enterprise and enterprising activities. More is expected of entrepreneurship scholars than in other disciplines because there is an expectation that they should perform across teaching, research and income generation streams. The pressures of the Research Excellence Framework (REF) can cause scholars to focus on their own output and on types of research that lend themselves to *REFability*. Many Centres-for-Entrepreneurship and Departments do not have the critical mass to perform trilatterly.

As a research community, it appears that Scottish entrepreneurship researchers have traditionally operated autonomously according to their individual research interests combined with the interests of writing partners within other Centres-for-Entrepreneurship research. This strong sense of independence is a particular characteristic of SER. This laissez-faire approach appears to have worked well and has allowed the development of distinctive research topics within the Centres. As vehicles for the perpetuation of entrepreneurship education, the Centres-for-Entrepreneurship have proven to be very effective. Although no one institution has developed a critical mass in terms of entrepreneurship research, collectively, such a diffused critical mass exists. Scotland and its universities fostered a homegrown cadre of entrepreneurship researchers who are, by and large, Scottish but international in outlook.

Hjorth (2008) identified three generations of Nordic entrepreneurship researchers, but in contemporary Scotland there are only two. The first are established Professors such as Alistair Anderson, Richard Harrison, Peter Rosa, Eleanor Shaw, Jonothan Levie, Sara Carter, Sarah Drakopoulou Dodd, Laura Galloway, Mike Danson, Sarah Cooper, Heather Fulford and the author, who populate the field and hold Chairs. A second generation of up-and-coming entrepreneurship researchers and scholars such as Geoff Whittam are continuing to establish a presence in the field but need to be encouraged and supported by their Business Schools and Universities by the creation of more Readers posts. Hjorth talked of the second generation of entrepreneurship researchers migrating from other academic disciplines such as economics, psychology and sociology. This in-migration has not occurred in Scotland. Instead, Scotland has developed a home-spun and close-knit network of entrepreneurship scholars for whom the discipline is their school of choice. SER is characterised by its focus on the qualitative aspects of entrepreneurship research. There appears to have been few inter-centre collaborations. Instead, scholars at each centre have developed a wide range of international collaborations.

The Future and Scotland's Entrepreneurial Ecosystem

Scotland's Centres-for-Entrepreneurship are part of a wider entrepreneurial ecosystem. Despite studies into ecosystem approaches proliferating the literature, the UK and Scottish HE sector is slow to adopt such practices. Ecosystems approaches offer new organisational forms and formations to emerge because the system is composed of components and linkages including universities (Zott et al. 2011). Entrepreneurship education in Scotland as an emergent, creative entrepreneurial ecosystem presents a supportive environment responsive to government policies (Stam 2014). O'Connor, in examining how entrepreneurship education meets government economic purposes, defined entrepreneurship as the "social process involving the efforts of individuals in activities that ultimately have economic implications at a regional and/or national level" (O'Connor 2013: 559). Entrepreneurship is socially embedded and ecosystems thrive on the social dynamics of entrepreneurship in framing the entrepreneur/scholar as a catalyst for economic activity (Bygrave and Minniti 2000). In this ecosystem, all the education providers should adopt a shared responsibility to nurture, encourage, support, fund, advise, facilitate and work for an entrepreneurial future for Scotland to produce a new generation of entrepreneurs and entrepreneurial ventures. This is a social and economic outcome desired by the Scottish Government through their policy inputs to underpin the creation, growth and flourishing of new firms and organisations to deliver desirable social and economic outcomes.

Universities as entrepreneurial institutions benefit from the breadth and depth of resources and capabilities and would benefit from being part of a wider entrepreneurial ecosystem (Rumelt 2005). The very notion of an ecosystem suggests that entrepreneurs have some degree of control over resources not under their control. An ecosystem embodies the interactions and interdependencies within industry value chains but goes beyond these to place emphasis on the concepts of an interdependent set of actors, governance and the enabling of entrepreneurial action (Adner and Kapoor 2010; Stam 2014). Entrepreneurial ecosystems approaches incorporate both agency and institutions into a system, but despite there being common characteristics among entrepreneurial ecosystems every system is different and idiosyncratic (Mason and Brown 2014) including the *Scottish School* which is an ecosystem in its own right. Entrepreneurial success in an ecosystems context is determined by the ability of entrepreneurs or entrepreneurial institutions to act as a transmission mechanism to advance the socio-economic fortunes of the place within which the entrepreneurial venturing happens. Such outputs can be academic as well as financial. The present 'Predators and Prey' system (Moore 1993) whereby all universities compete against each other for students and funding is wasteful and needs to change. From a student and customer focus, it is evident that many of the existing Centres-for-Entrepreneurship offer similar modules limiting student choice. This is an opportunity to further specialise in their degree course and module contents, to differentiate themselves and attract higher student numbers. In a Scottish context, this entails following the REAP Scotland/MIT Entrepreneurial Eco-System Model to author a more entrepreneurial Scotland to achieve a collective impact by increasing innovation-driven entrepreneurship in Scotland (REAP Undated). It makes more sense to adopt an ecosystem model for research and commercialisation projects as many Centres-for-Entrepreneurship are competing for the same research and commercialisation monies.

There are collaborative models one should seriously consider adopting to increase the chances of success in research and income-generation activities.

- In Policing Research, the mass of policing scholars in Scotland was quite substantial, yet diversely ineffective. The creation of the Scottish Institute for Policing Research (SIPR) circa 2006 led to a renaissance and collaboration in terms of policing research, which is the envy of other countries globally. Creating SIPR, to which eight Scottish Universities signed up to, encouraged scholars from individual universities to collaborate on research and income-generating projects. Clients approach SIPR with their research needs and, through their database of research specialists, SIPRs help individual scholars and universities to benefit from research income, acting as an honest broker and a guarantor of research quality. The SIPR model is one which the SER community would benefit from. Although there are existing agencies and entities, such as the SIE, they are more focused on practice.
- Another collaborative model worthy of consideration is the Research Alliance Model, currently being practised by the N8 Research Group in the north of England which acts collaboratively, sharing knowledge and expertise in research, drawing on available researchers from across the eight universities. This model could be used as a template for Scottish Centres-for-Entrepreneurship to follow.

Without such serious collaboration, there is a danger that the globally renowned excellence of Scottish scholars will be lost. Many such scholars are reaching the end of their careers and Emeritus status, and unless positive affirmative action is taken, they may not be replaced by a new generation. That would be a great loss.

Another salient issue relates to the politics of UK Business Schools and how the research landscape has been changed by the 'age of austerity' and by REF politics. The recession of 2007 hit the university sector heavily, and in many Business Schools led to an initial round of voluntary redundancies and an increase in teaching hours for remaining staff. The fractious REF politics of the 2007 and 2013 Research Exercise Assessment (REA) and REF saw an increase in the awareness of publishing in top-tier journals. As Entrepreneurship, as an academic discipline, is poorly served by a low number of such journals, the task of publishing at a high level is made more difficult. The insistence of many universities on not allowing staff to publish unless the article appears in three- or four-star journal discourages research. The continuing recession was further exacerbated in the post-REF 2013 period by a reduction in research funding to Business Schools considered to be underperforming. The net result may lead to a reduction in the number of active entrepreneurship researchers. Unless individual Schools, and their Centres-for-Entrepreneurship, adapt to the situation, then closures seem likely. If individual Chairs are not replaced, there will be less opportunities for ambitious researchers to develop their careers in Scotland and could lead to an exodus of talent to other parts of the UK or abroad. This is not intended as being alarmist, but merely inevitable, without increased funding.

Another facet of the changing face of Entrepreneurial Education in the UK and Scottish higher education system is the conflation with enterprise in its widest sense, income generation and commercialisation with Entrepreneurship per se, whereby there is an expectation that Professors of Entrepreneurship should possess high-level commercialisation and income-generation skills. There has been a rise in the number of job adverts where Entrepreneurship Professors are required to have enterprise development experience. The skill sets are not interchangeable and very few Entrepreneurship Professors possess this duality. Many positions remain unfilled. This points to a need for a dual career path for future Entrepreneurship Professors to differentiate between academic researchers and practical income generators. There is a need to protect and nurture the next generation of entrepreneurship researchers.

The initiation and development of a Scottish Institute for Entrepreneurship Research and Excellence would fit in with the developing notion of an Entrepreneurial Scotland and its plethora of enterprise-based agencies and networks which form a naturally occurring ecosystem.[ii] Of particular interest are 'The Entrepreneurial Exchange', 'Entrepreneurial Scotland' and the 'Saltire Foundation' (Smith and Warren 2016). The *Scottish School* must be viewed as part of this wider system and Scotland's 'World Leading "Can Do" Culture'. There is an air of change. There is the collaboration between 'The Saltire Foundation' and the 'Babson-Kauffmann Centre-for-Entrepreneurship' in the USA whereby the Foundation sponsors and supports Scottish Business people to gain an Executive education. Yet, we have a significant pool of world-class entrepreneurship talent in Scotland. There are contemporary developments. At UWS, the 'Enterprise Academy' concept focuses on the practical and not on research. Likewise, Dundee University has announced the opening of a new Centre for Entrepreneurship in conjunction with 'Elevator' with the emphasis on the practical and income-generation sides of enterprise.[iii] The plan is to emulate the existing new Aberdeen 'Elevator' Centre for Entrepreneurship.[iv] This has implications for academic Entrepreneurship-Research-Centres (McEwan 2015). A new more integrated approach is required to capitalise on the gains of the Scottish School assisted by embracing an entrepreneurial ecosystem approach.

This entails constructing and protecting a viable and sustainable network of entrepreneurship centres with a focus on supporting entrepreneurship research. One should reconsider the legacy and the future of SER to build upon the momentum of the early 1990s. Individually and collectively, first-generation Scottish scholars have developed and fostered a climate where entrepreneurship research flourishes because of its Centres-of-Entrepreneurship. First-generation researchers, Readers, Professors and Chairs are at the pinnacle of their careers and contribute individually and collectively to SER research output and to the wider entrepreneurship community as Editors and Reviewers, for example, Alistair Anderson with ERD. So much so that Professor Peter Rosa credited Professor Anderson as having initiated the '*Aberdeen School*' of Entrepreneurship research because of his efficacy in developing entrepreneurship research and researchers.

A new generation of Lecturers, Senior Lecturers and Readers are emerging behind them but will there be Centres-of-Entrepreneurship for them to inherit and run? It is vital that a new National entrepreneurship research strategy be developed and that existing Centres receive fresh funding and impetus. Otherwise, when the first-generation researchers retire there is a possibility that their pioneering work will be lost. There is a danger driven by REF research politics and austerity measures that when existing Chairs retire the Centres may be wound down and the research staff subsumed within the management sections of Business Schools. This would be a grave mistake. The government policy of initiating the Scottish Centres-for-Entrepreneurship has obviously transformed the entrepreneurship education and research landscapes in Scotland over the past three decades.

5.3 Conclusions and Assessing the Impact

The early years of the planned strategy were characterised by inter-centre cross-fertilisation of staff. The planned consortium approach worked well but has waned over the years as individual Centres developed an autonomous presence. There has been a reduction in the number and presence of active Centres. Individually no one Centre has developed a critical mass although the Hunter Centre comes close. Although there are few inter-centre research collaborations, collectively there is a critical mass of entrepreneurship scholars with in excess of forty Scottish Entrepreneurship Scholars identified. The collective research output of the *Scottish School* is the key achievement of the Scottish Centres-for-Entrepreneurship. This chapter has documented and evidenced their collective efficacy and highlighted lessons learnt in the process. It also identifies possible future approaches for entrepreneurship centres from the perspective of potential implications for policy and practice for HEIs. To assess the impact of the notion of the *Scottish School* will require further study.

A sense of what constitutes *Scottishness* has been gained in a SER context and has gained fresh insights into the phenomenon through salient observations based on this research. SER represents a very active field of research manifested as a broad range of topics published in a widespread of journals. This study demonstrates that like the situation described by Hjorth in Scandinavia between 1995 and 2005, Scotland collectively developed a critical mass of entrepreneurship scholars within the area, albeit with a diffused critical mass.

There is not an all-encompassing, unified Scottish Entrepreneurship Research Strategy, albeit Scotland hosted Babson 2004 and ISBE 2007 and 2015, and the Annual Entrepreneurship Conference is still flourishing. Nevertheless, it is a success story worth telling. But how will it be told? Obviously this chapter is a beginning, but a funded study would accelerate the process. There is a need to consolidate and celebrate the success of the *Scottish School* and to plan for the next two decades. A rebranding of the SER effort is needed. The author's observations presented earlier reflect upon a history and sociality in Scotland characterised by a cultural attitude of equal opportunities for all and have consequences for Entrepreneurship Research. Entrepreneurial activity has become a focus for state design, as in the Nordic countries. This desire of the state to stimulate the populations' entrepreneurial behaviour has to be balanced with the lingering perception of Scotland as an anti-entrepreneurial culture.

Nonetheless, Scotland has produced a considerable pool of talent in terms of entrepreneurship researchers and the existing Centres-for-Entrepreneurship still have an influential role to play in the development of entrepreneurship in Scotland. Scotland must continue to grow second- and third-generation homegrown entrepreneurship scholars to continue in the tradition already established. There is a pressing need to develop a more cohesive interface between Scottish entrepreneurship researchers and policymakers and to better understand and embrace an entrepreneurial ecosystem approach and engage with each other to create the context to enhance future research. As entrepreneurial universities and institutions, they must operate entrepreneurially and engage with the discovery and/or creation and development of opportunities. Universities should continue to grow and have an effect at the social and economic levels within their region or specific place.

There are obvious limitations to this reflection, which only considers the universities and not the Further Education sector/Colleges which play an important part in the Scottish entrepreneurial education system. Given the acknowledged trend towards delivering a more practical entrepreneurial education, it is evident that colleges cannot be excluded from the debate, nor can the Enterprise Development Sector. Many new Scottish universities subsumed parts of the college system into their structure and their management and enterprise lecturers have their background in further, not higher, education. Many of these dedicated lecturers do not possess a doctorate and do not have a penchant for research and writing academic papers. Obviously this is a generalisation, but, nevertheless, there is a place for academically orientated Centres-for-Entrepreneurship.

This study has implications for policymakers in government and quasi-governmental institutions involved in the promotion of entrepreneurship. This chapter has introduced the notions of SER and the *Scottish School* as a concept in Entrepreneurship and Management circles highlighting a pressing need for a new ecology of Scottish Enterprise education and provision, and Scottish universities need a new business model based on innovative ecosystems models (Rennings 2000; Zott et al. 2011). Having presented a possible vision for the future, it is necessary to conduct further research to document the achievements of the first-generation researchers by conducting empirical research.[v] There is considerable scope for a new consortium approach to be initiated and we as a Scottish Entrepreneurship Community need to protect our legacy and develop it for future posterity.

Notes

i. Namely the University of the Highlands and Islands; University of Aberdeen; Robert Gordon University, Aberdeen; University of Abertay, Dundee; Dundee University; University of St Andrew's; University of Edinburgh;

Edinburgh Napier University; Heriot-Watt University; Queen Margaret University, Edinburgh; University of Stirling; University of Glasgow; University of Strathclyde; Glasgow Caledonian University; University of the West of Scotland; Glasgow School of Art; Royal Conservatoire Scotland; Scotland's Rural College; and The Open University.

ii. These include national agencies and initiatives such as Scottish Enterprise; Highlands & Islands Enterprise; Business Gateway; Federation of Small Businesses Scotland; Scottish Chambers of Commerce; Skills Development Scotland; Chartered Management Institute; The Entrepreneurial Exchange; Scottish Institute for Enterprise; MIT Regional Entrepreneurship Acceleration Program (REAP); Cooperative Development Scotland; Innovation Scotland Forum; Social Enterprise Academy; Micro Tyco; Scottish Edge; PSYBT; Royal Society of Edinburgh; SE/RSE Enterprise Fellowship; CeeD; Interface/Voluntary Action Scotland; Bridge 2 Business; Converge Challenge; Power of Youth; We Can Scotland; Universities Scotland; Linc Scotland; SenScot; Innovate Scotland; Youth Business Scotland; Youth Enterprise Scotland; Disabled Entrepreneurs Network; Entrepreneurial Scotland; Women's Enterprise Scotland; RBS Centre for Entrepreneurs; The Saltire Foundation and Resilient Scotland. Regional initiatives include Enterprise Campus; Elevator; Creative Clyde; Paisley-In-Cube; Entrepreneurial Spark; Glasgow Social Enterprise Network and Barrhead Foundry.

iii. See http://www.sbnn.co.uk/2016/04/07/new-centre-of-entrepreneurship-revealed-at-university-of-dundee/.

iv. See http://www.elevatoruk.com/centre-for-entrepreneurship/the-centre/.

v. This will entail embarking upon a study of the Scottish School of Entrepreneurship Research. This is crucial to our understanding what is special about SER and why it should be encouraged. To achieve this understanding, it will be necessary to draw upon published SER in journal publications to identify themes, trends and tendencies, and consider the phenomenon in a broader sociohistorical perspective. From this, it will be possible to identify distinct schools of entrepreneurship researchers and suggest directions for the future development of this distinctive 'Scottish School' of Entrepreneurship Research. It is anticipated that this will be facilitated by applying for a research grant to the Carnegie Trust for Scotland.

References

Adner, R., & Kapoor, R. (2010). Value creation in innovation ecosystems: How the structure of technological interdependence affects firm performance in new technology generations. *Strategic Management Journal, 31*, 306–333.

Bygrave, W., & Minniti, M. (2000). The social dynamics of entrepreneurship'. *Entrepreneurship Theory & Practice*, *24*(3), 25–36.
Checkland, S. G. (1976). *The Upas tree: Glasgow 1875–1975: A study in growth and contraction*. Glasgow: The University of Glasgow Press.
Down, S. (2013). The distinctiveness of the European tradition in entrepreneurship research. *Entrepreneurship and Regional Development: An International Journal*, *25*(1–2), 1–4.
Hjorth, D. (2008). Nordic entrepreneurship research. *Entrepreneurship Theory & Practice*, *32*(2), 313–338.
Lave, J., & Wenger, E. (1991). *Situated learning: Legitimate peripheral participation*. Cambridge: Cambridge University Press.
Making it Happen: Enterprise and Entrepreneurship Education. http://www.universities-scotland.ac.uk/uploads/US%20Making%20It%20Happen%20Nov2015.pdf.
Maniukiewicz, C., Williams, S., & Keogh, W. (1999). Partnerships and networks: Lessons from facilitating entrepreneurship. *Journal of Small Business and Enterprise Development*, *6*(1), 68–79.
Mason, C., & Brown, R. (2014). *Entrepreneurial ecosystems and growth oriented entrepreneurship*. Paper prepared for a workshop of the OECD LEED Programme and the Dutch Ministry of Economic Affairs, The Hague, Netherlands, 7th November 2013.
McEwan, G. (2015). Delivering entrepreneurship training and support. *Local Economy*, *30*(5), 568–576.
McCrone, D. (2001). *Understanding Scotland: The sociology of a nation*. London: Routledge.
Moore, J. F. (1993). Predators and prey: A new ecology of competition. *Harvard Business Review*, May-June, 75–86.
Muncey, T. (2010). *Creating autoethnographies*. London: Sage.
O'Connor, A. (2013). A conceptual framework for entrepreneurship education policy: Meeting government and economic purposes. *Journal of Business Venturing*, *28*, 546–563.
REAP Scotland. (Undated). *Increasing innovation-driven entrepreneurship in Scotland through Collective Impact*. Report.
Rennings, K. (2000). Redefining innovation—Eco-innovation research and the contribution from ecological economics. *Ecological Economics*, *32*(2), 319–332.
Rumelt, R. P. (2005). Theory strategy entrepreneurship. In S. A. Alvarez, R. Agarwal, & O. Sorenson (Eds.), International handbook series on entrepreneurship, *Handbook of entrepreneurship research interdisciplinary perspectives*. Vol. 2. New York: Springer.
Scottish Enterprise (1997). Local Heroes Report.

Smith, R. (2012). *Scottish entrepreneurship research*. Paper presented at an ISBE Seminar on Scottish Entrepreneurship Research at The University of the West of Scotland.

Smith, R. (2016). *Celebrating 'The Scottish School of Entrepreneurship Research' and the emergence of an eco-sphere approach to delivering entrepreneurship education in the 21st century*. An Inaugural Lecture, University of the West of Scotland, March, 2016.

Smith, R., & Warren, L. (2016). Visualising representations of the entrepreneurial exchange: Considering images of entrepreneurial organizing and identity. Working paper.

Stam, E., (2014). The Dutch entrepreneurial ecosystem. July 29, 2014.

Williams, S., & Turnbull, A., (1997). *First moves into entrepreneurship teaching in Scottish universities; a consortium approach*. http://www.sbaer.uca.edu/research/icsb/1997/90.pdf.

Zott, C., Amit, R., & Massa, L. (2011). The business model: Recent developments and future research. Online First *Journal of Management, 37*(4), 1019–1042.

Websites

http://www.entrepreneurship-scotland.com
http://www.entrepreneurialexchange.com

Robert Smith is Professor of Enterprise and Innovation at the University of the West of Scotland, Dumfries. He has a dual role as Professor of Business Intelligence at 'The Crichton Institute', Dumfries. His research interests include entrepreneurial leadership, rural and criminal entrepreneurship, entrepreneurial narrative, entrepreneurial identity, as well as small and family business. He has taught Leadership at MBA level, 'Entrepreneurial Leadership' at undergraduate level and Police Leadership at Masters level as well as 'Strategy into Action' at DBA level. Robert has over 150 peer-reviewed publications in journals and book chapters.

PART III

European, Canadian and African Entrepreneurship Centres

In Part III of this book, two case studies of universities in Spain (EDEM Business School and Santander International Entrepreneurship Centre, University of Cantabria), one from Canada (the Hunter Centre for Entrepreneurship and Innovation) and one from Ghana (Centre for Entrepreneurship and Small Enterprises Development, University of Cape Coast) are discussed. Specific areas to identify in the following three case studies are as follows:

- EDEM Business School (Chapter 6): the involvement of businesses in the development of strategies and structures; the existence of an integrated ecosystem; measuring the worth of their programmes.
- Santander International Entrepreneurship Centre (Chapter 7): the importance of an entrepreneurial ecosystem; addressing the specific challenges of their environment.
- The Hunter Centre for Entrepreneurship and Innovation (Chapter 8): the innovative corporate strategy; buying in from senior leaders in the university; caution not to focus too narrowly only on start-ups and new venture creation.
- Centre for Entrepreneurship and Small Enterprises Development (Chapter 9): addressing new markets nationally and internationally; pioneering role of centre within the context of the university.

It is clear from discussions that an innovative corporate strategy should guide the activities of these centres and that sizable investments are needed to enable these centres to scale up their activities.

CHAPTER 6

EDEM Business School (Spain)

Martina Luckanicova and Andrea Conchado

Abstract Marina de Empresas (MdE) is a unique space consisting out of an entrepreneurial hub whose aim is that of supporting the full entrepreneurial cycle through the three entities of which it is comprised: EDEM Business School for education and training, Lanzadera for acceleration and Angels for investment. The new shared location in Valencia's MdE offers a comprehensive initiative that brings all the stages involved in starting up a business and promoting a common philosophy based on leadership, promotion of sustainable enterprises and the culture of endeavour together. In this case study, evidence was provided of how activities contribute in terms of acquiring teamwork skills, time management, working under pressure and project management skills, in addition to acquiring a feeling of commitment towards their colleagues. In addition, the authors found a potential area for improvement related to the link between the academic curriculum and its application in the cross-curricular project. These findings have

---

M. Luckanicova
EDEM Business School, Valencia, Spain
e-mail: mluckanicova@edem.es

A. Conchado
EDEM Business School and the Universidad Politécnica de Valencia,
Valencia, Spain
e-mail: aconchado@edem.es

© The Author(s) 2017
G. Maas, P. Jones (eds.), *Entrepreneurship Centres*,
DOI 10.1007/978-3-319-47892-0_6

important implications for pursuing alternative courses of action in order to find a meaningful link between theory and practice.

Keywords Entrepreneurship · Leadership · Training · Sustainable enterprises · Endeavour

6.1 Introduction

Entrepreneurial activity is linked to the individual perception of an opportunity and the ability to put it in place, along with satisfactory macroeconomic conditions in the surrounding environment (Fernández-Laviada 2014). Thus, in accordance with the 'revised GEM conceptual framework', an adequate social and political-economic context, individual motivation and the skills and expertise needed to carry out the entrepreneurial activity must all exist in order to enhance the entrepreneurial output (new jobs and value creation). *Marina de Empresas* (MdE) is a unique space where all these conditions converge in a major Mediterranean-area entrepreneurial hub whose aim is that of supporting the full entrepreneurial cycle through the three entities of which it is comprised: EDEM Business School for education and training, Lanzadera for acceleration and Angels for investment. After a number of years growing and developing independently, these three pillars for nurturing individual initiative and talent are now located together within one space. The new shared location in Valencia's MdE offers a comprehensive initiative that brings all the stages involved in starting up a business and promoting a common philosophy based on leadership, promotion of sustainable enterprises and the culture of endeavour together (see Fig. 6.1). Furthermore, facilitating access not only to training and mentoring but also to venture capital is highly valuable, especially in the context of Spanish culture. In total, thanks to the accelerator Lanzadera, which has now been active for three years, 140 jobs have been created and 87 % of the start-ups supported have managed to stay afloat. At any rate, the emergence of MdE provides the opportunity for creating new and fresh synergies.

EDEM was founded more than thirteen years ago under the auspices of the local Valencian Business Association (AVE). The school was originally focused on the development of specific leadership skills, and with time, it has evolved to what it is today, a Business School attended by younger and older students alike (there are around 1,000 students enrolled every year). The school's trustees and members are prestigious

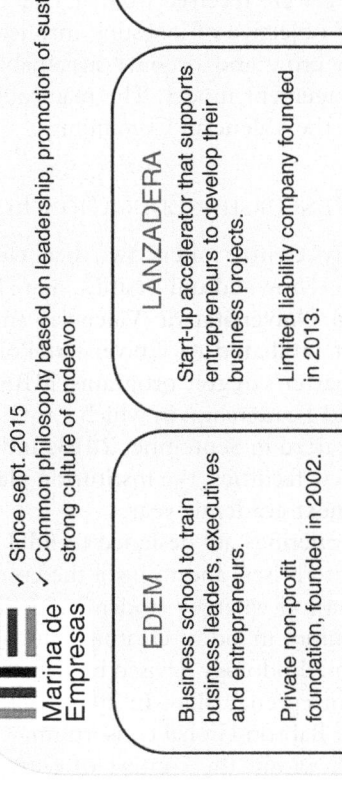

Fig. 6.1 Marina de Empresas: Its pillars and main figures

companies that play an important role in the local and national economy, and they are also actively involved in the centre's life, which represents an enormous added value.

As an accelerator, Lanzadera offers much support and a wide range of resources, such as personalised training courses, mentoring, best practices and sharing knowledge on proven business models, administrative support, physical premises and facilities and networking and financing. In addition, entrepreneurs have access to a collateral-free loan at an interest rate of EURIBOR +0 %, whose eligibility depends on the specific needs of each project and the milestones achieved. To gain access to the space in such lucrative conditions, the projects must overcome a highly demanding selection. The rate of acceptance for the last three years stood at around 1 %, and almost 6,700 applications were received from all over Spain.

Angels was created with the objective of investing into leaders (companies) in order to help them grow and become sustainable, applying proven Spanish successful management model. The main objective is to stimulate the business sector in the Valencian Community.

6.2 EDEM's Entrepreneurship Education Ecosystem

Currently, EDEM's University Centre offers two bachelor's degree programmes, both affiliated to renowned universities, namely a BBA in Entrepreneurship (affiliated to Universitat de Valencia) and a BSc in Engineering and Management (affiliated to Universitat Politécnica de Valencia), in addition to two master's degree programs, MBA junior and Master in Entrepreneurship and Leadership, in which a total number of 274 students are enrolled. It started in September 2015, and coinciding with the inauguration of the new facilities, the institution plans to grow by approximately 30 % in the next academic year.

All of EDEM's educational offerings are designed to fulfil the present and future needs of business enterprises, and to instil the entrepreneurial spirit, which is defined as a method whereby students practice creating, finding and acting on opportunities in aid of creating value (Neck et al. 2014), in accordance with the methodology devised by Babson College, a global reference for teaching entrepreneurship. In 2014, EDEM became the first Spanish member of the Babson Global consortium.

According to Brush (2012), within the context of entrepreneurship education ecosystem (EEE), universities need to consider three variables, namely curriculum, co-curricular activities and research, as well as to

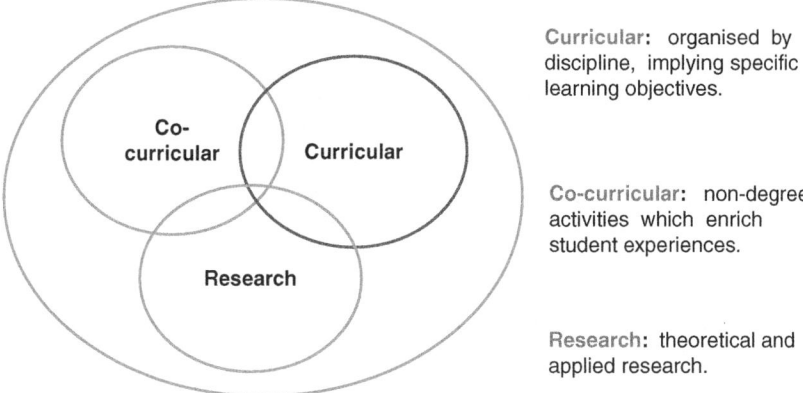

Fig. 6.2 Domains of entrepreneurship education ecosystem (*Source*: Brush 2012.)

promote cross-campus entrepreneurial activities and to nest them within the community and school (see Fig. 6.2).

In EDEM, the three EEE domains are closely related to the pillars of MdE, as shown in Fig. 6.3. EDEM's educational model is based on the development of personal skills, attitudes and values, encouraging students to act in situations of uncertainty and minimising fear of failure. Students learn within a specific business vision encompassing five factors (client, employee, supplier, society and capital).

The participants of the senior programmes (executives and professionals) take an active role in the whole ecosystem through different activities, for example, running workshops with students to share experiences, offering scholarships for the best applicant, enabling students to visit their companies and to see the application of the knowledge areas, summer internships, teaching at university centre and mentoring student entrepreneurial activities.

Lanzadera is also actively involved in student life, carrying out joint activities among students and start-ups in the accelerator. Win-win solutions are created between these two groups in different situations: students participate in testing minimum viable products, brainstorming and knowledge-sharing. Moreover, professional mentors from Lanzadera offer quality feedback for entrepreneurial projects created by students; there are also a number of competitions being organised on campus, and the best students are allowed to carry out their internship in Lanzadera's start-ups.

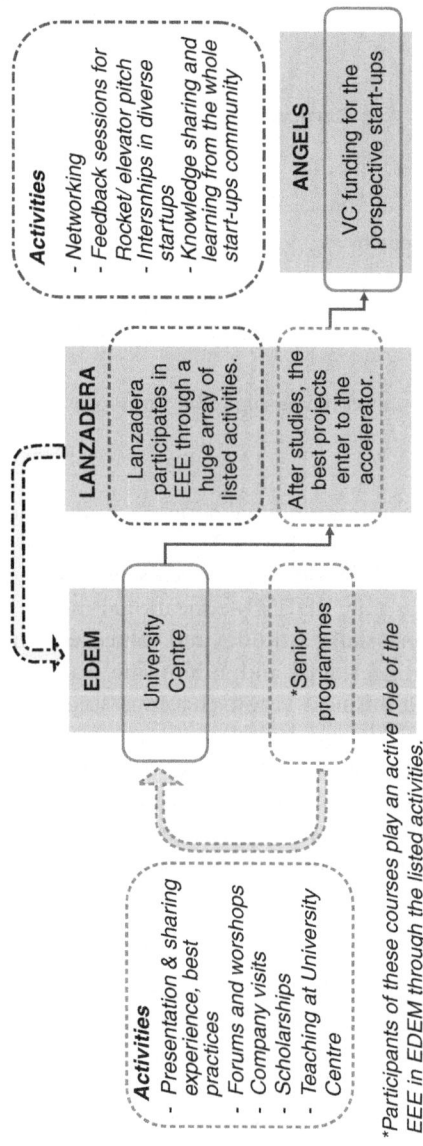

Fig. 6.3 Entrepreneurship education ecosystem in Marina de Empresas

Finally, Angels is a vital part of the whole ecosystem as without it there would be no financial support for the most viable projects. In addition, professional investment managers from Angels also act as tutors for students.

Being surrounded by a community such as this, providing constant professional feedback derives in having a solid knowledge base, as well as in favourable networking opportunities for students. 2016 produced the first BBA graduates, and 85 % will continue with entrepreneurial activities, 40 % have been accepted by Lanzadera to work on their start-up projects, 14 % are involved in family businesses and 31 % are interested in intrapreneurship.

Table 6.1 offers a detailed review of entrepreneurial activities organised by EDEM's University Centre for undergraduate studies considering three dimensions of EEE (Brush 2012).

The 2015–2016 academic year has seen the launch of the new cross-curricular project aimed at first-year students enrolled in the BSc in Engineering and Management. The aim was to promote higher levels of learning, as well as fostering student self-confidence through their involvement in decision-making processes (Blumenfeld et al. 1991). According to Thomas (2000), this project may be considered a project-based learning (PBL) activity as it involves inquiry, knowledge building and resolution, underpinned by a certain level of difficulty that ensures the need for constructive investigation. Thus, EDEM opted for an entrepreneurial/business-oriented PBL activity as a key component of the engineering programme, in order that the students could acquire a more in-depth understanding of the scientific and technological concepts, while putting them into practice, as well as to experience intrapersonal communication as a necessary aspect of entrepreneurial practice (Botha 2010). There have been a number of positive initiatives using this methodology in engineering programmes (Frank et al. 2003; Hadim and Esche 2002; Lehmann et al. 2008). In the following section, the successful application of this methodology will be discussed for the development of an entrepreneurial orientation among first-year students.

6.3 The Cross-Curricular Project

There were 30 students enrolled in the first year of the BSc in Business and Engineering, 25 of whom participated in the study (interview), so the sampling error was considered low enough for developing a cross-sectional study (8 %). Data was collected in May 2016, coinciding with the end of

Table 6.1 Entrepreneurial activities in BBA and BSc

	BBA in Entrepreneurship	BSc in Engineering and Management

Curricular	• Bachelor's degree in business administration, specialised in entrepreneurship
	• Four-year study
	• Studies divided into three main blocks:
	  ○ Specific knowledge from business area
	  ○ Business model of five components
	  ○ Managerial skill
		• Bachelor's degree in Engineering and Management, first of its kind in Spain
		• Four-year study
		• Studies divided into three main blocks:
		  ○ 30 % technology subjects
		  ○ 24 % basic science
		  ○ 46 % business and management

Co-curricular	• Entrepreneurial project where students work in groups from the beginning of their studies, with ongoing support and feedback from Lanzadera and EDEM professors	• Cross-curricular project that promotes teamworking by the students and involves overcoming a challenge defined by EDEM by applying knowledge learnt in (and outside) class
	• Workshops to develop and enhance soft skills: emotional intelligence, time management, communication skills, creativity, conflict management, negotiation skills, leadership and project/change management • Company visits and talks by entrepreneurs and executives • A tutorial action plan in conjunction with a professional coach who helps achieve the academic and business objectives • Yearly internships (national and international) including individual tracking • Bilingual lectures: in English and Spanish (50–50 %) • Competitions on best entrepreneurial project, idea and business model • Internships in Lanzadera • Volunteering for local-level social activities (e.g. organising marathons in Valencia) • Approaching reality through the practical experiences of professors (70 % are entrepreneurs, executives and professionals, and 30 % are acknowledged academically rigorous professors) • Colloquiums with acknowledged academic and professional figures (e.g. Nobel Prize laureate for economics in 2015 Prof Anton Deaton) • Entrepreneurial classroom – official opening in October 2016	

the 2015/2016 academic year. Overall, 28 % of students were women ($N = 7$) and the average age was 19.7 (SD = 2.2). None of these students had parents (mother or father) running their own business, although 16 % ($N = 4$) of them had started work on their own project.

Teaching innovation consisted of a cross-curricular PBL activity, and the results were presented in the form of an end-of-year competition. The following outcome was expected in terms of learning:

- Experiencing teamwork and all that it entails (effective communication, problem-solving and time management)
- Enhancing motivation for knowledge building and searching for relevant information
- Consolidating knowledge of theoretical concepts, through its application in real problem-solving

Students were expected to make a toy remote control boat by applying the concepts learnt in the subjects included in the first course:

- First semester: calculus, chemistry, physics I, business and computer science
- Second semester: physics II, algebra, differential equations, biology, graphic expression and economics

Professors who taught each of these subjects suggested a number of activities related to the different stages involved in building the boat. These activities were defined in the subject's syllabus and assigned a 10 % score that counted towards the final assessment in the subject.

Students were grouped into four-people teams formed according to two criteria: (1) heterogeneity within each team and (2) homogeneity between teams. In addition, the individual preferences of the students were not considered for team compositions.

The procedure for the implementation of the activity was carried out in different stages: firstly, an introductory session took place at the start of the course, the aim being to encourage participation and define schedules and learning outcomes. Subsequently, each professor explained the activity in relation to the deliverables planned for their subjects. Throughout the course, professors provided guidance and attended coordination meetings in order to monitor the evolution of the project and control possible deviations concerning the project management triangle (scope, time and cost). At the end of the course, the students presented their results to an audience while being evaluated by an academic board. The evaluation considered the achievements at team level. After their presentations, they were invited to present their toy remote control boat on the water outside.

The final evaluation took into account both the presentation of the team and the feasibility of the outcome, which in this case was the prototype.

6.4 Methodology

Student satisfaction in relation to learning outcomes was measured using an ad hoc scale, including six items related to teamwork, knowledge acquisition (search for information), knowledge application (the comprehension and application of theoretical concepts) and overall satisfaction with the PBL method. Responses to this scale were scored using a five-point Likert-type scale ranging from 1 (very unsatisfied) to 5 (very satisfied). Similarly, entrepreneurial orientation of university students was rated using the scale developed and validated by Bolton and Lane (2012). This scale includes 12 items structured into three factors: (1) risk-taking, (2) innovation and (3) proactiveness. Responses were measured using a five-point Likert-type scale, ranging from 1 (low) to 5 (high). The cross-curricular project's contribution towards the development of this entrepreneurial orientation was assessed using a reflective self-evaluation approach. Students were asked to assess the percentage development of the selected skills according to their own perception by evaluating themselves before and after the project, where 0 % meant there had been no contribution at all. Innovation was defined as seeking new solutions to problems and tackling new projects; risk-taking as the planning of scenarios to overcome challenges in projects and considering back-up plans for them; and proactiveness as taking the initiative, proposing and implementing improvements and taking responsibility for moving the projects forward. Descriptive statistics were taken into account for both scales: measuring satisfaction in regards to the project's learning outcomes and entrepreneurial orientation. From a qualitative point of view, the reflections provided by students about the teaching innovation (cross-curricular project) were thematically analysed using a top-down approach. Strong and weak points of the activity were identified and discussed in terms of its success in helping students to acquire and/or develop new skills.

6.5 Results

Satisfaction with Cross-Curricular Project

Table 6.2 shows the average satisfaction in relation to items covered in the cross-curricular project. The highest score was defined as "I understood

Table 6.2 Satisfaction in relation to the cross-curricular PBL activity: descriptive statistics

Item category	Item description	Mean	SD
Teamwork	I understood my role as a team member, as well as the role of my colleagues	3.80	0.77
Teamwork	We took decisions together and chose solutions for each problem by consensus	3.40	0.94
Overall satisfaction with the PBL	I enjoyed the project-based learning, rather than traditional lessons	3.30	1.03
Knowledge acquisition	It has been a motivational activity for searching information	3.25	1.16
Teamwork	I felt comfortable working in teams	3.25	1.07
Knowledge application	It helped me to understand the theoretical concepts studied in the classroom	2.65	0.81

my role as a team member, as well as the role of my colleagues" and the lowest score as "It helped me to understand the theoretical concepts studied in the classroom".

After thematically analysing the students´ reflections on their experience, the authors concluded that almost all of them reported that they had developed their teamwork abilities as a result of completing their projects. Above all, they reported increased awareness in regards to the need for tolerance and respect towards others, as well as the need for internal coordination and negotiation with others in order to arrive at agreements:

"Although things go wrong sometimes, you have to keep going. There are always different opinions in the teams, but the aim is to find and reach an agreement. In the end, the problems are solved more satisfactorily when solved within the team".

"We have learned that problems may be successfully solved if you work productively with your team".

"It is vital to understand the role of each member of the team in order to adequately coordinate and collaborate".

Other competences that were widely reported as having been positive the students´ learning experience were in relation to time management, working under pressure and project management, all of which are linked to the commitment/motivation to move the project forward:

"Working in teams is a complex issue. Therefore, it is essential to devise a good plan in order to work calmly and achieve the required level of commitment".

"I felt obliged to do my best to overcome our problems, even though it entailed working under pressure".

"In order to run the project and overcome the initial difficulties, we had to search for alternative solutions all the time. Even though we failed at the beginning, we found a way to redefine our trajectory".

Furthermore, student reflections about the aforementioned project revealed a comprehensive improvement where their planning skills were concerned. These assessments are in line with previous research as this methodology has been described as a time-consuming activity for constructing personally meaningful artefacts (Grant 2002). Suggestions as to how this project could be improved for the future were mainly based on redefining some activities within specific subjects, where the link with the theoretical concepts was perceived as insufficient. This is understandable as students tend to optimise their time at university and activities of a co-curricular nature require more preparation and time. In addition, one of the objectives of the cross-curricular project was to encourage students to perform knowledge building (searching more information and knowledge and its application). Perhaps instead of this, motivational mechanisms should be exercised and more reflection activities could be carried out in order to support the general understanding and meaning of the project. In addition, students also reported that on occasion they felt neglected, and that they would have preferred to have received more guidance from their mentors-teachers. In their own words, they felt some degree of entitlement in this respect on account of being young first-year students. However, entrepreneurial learning involves experiencing uncertainty, proactiveness and risk-taking (Bolton and Lane 2012), so it is debatable whether more attention from the professors would encourage or restrict the experiencing of the aforementioned behavioural factors.

"The project would be better if tasks were defined with regard to the theoretical knowledge we studied in the classroom".

"The rules for the development of the project should be defined from the very beginning of the course (limit of budget, team composition, resources, limitations...)".

"We felt that some professors suggested activities that were completely disconnected from their contents. These subjects should not be present in future editions".

Entrepreneurial Orientation of Students

Generally, students reported very high, strong entrepreneurial orientation within all items of the categories studied, as proposed by Bolton and Lane (2012) (see Table 6.3), distributing the means almost homogenously. Nevertheless, the highest scoring item was "I am willing to invest a lot of time and/or money on something that might yield a high return" associated with the perception of risk-taking, and the lowest score was that of the item associated with proactiveness: "I tend to plan ahead for projects". The means by categories allocate the factors to the following items: (1) risk-taking, (2) innovation and (3) proactiveness.

Table 6.3 Individual entrepreneurial orientation: descriptive statistics

Item category (factor)	Item description	Mean	SD
Risk-taking	I am willing to invest a lot of time and/or money on something that might yield a high return	4.56	0.51
Proactiveness	I prefer to 'step-up' and get things going on projects rather than sit and wait for someone else to do it	4.40	0.58
Innovation	I favour experimentation and original approaches to problem-solving rather than using methods others generally use for solving their problems	4.24	0.93
Innovation	I often like to try new and unusual activities that are not typical but not necessarily risky	4.20	0.71
Risk-taking	I like to take bold actions by venturing into the unknown	4.12	0.73
Risk-taking	I tend to act 'boldly' in situations where risk is involved	4.08	0.57
Innovation	I prefer to try my own unique way when learning new things rather than doing it like everyone else does	3.96	0.93
Proactiveness	I usually act in anticipation of future problems, needs or changes	3.92	0.64
Innovation	In general, where projects are concerned, I prefer a strong emphasis on unique, one-of-a-kind approaches rather than revisiting tried and tested approaches	3.80	0.76
Proactiveness	I tend to plan ahead for projects	3.72	0.84

Table 6.4 Progress in entrepreneurial orientation

Item category (factor)	Mean of individual assessment of students in each factor	Individual self-perception of how the cross-curricular project helped to develop the factors (%)
Risk-taking	4.3	57
Innovation	4.1	63
Proactiveness	4.0	66

Additionally, the self-perception of students in terms of their progress in regards to the aforementioned Entrepreneurial Orientation factors relating to working on cross-curricular projects was positive, proactiveness coming first at 66 % improvement. Perceived improvement in the attitude to preference for innovation was evaluated at 63 % and attitude to risk-taking scored 57 % (see Table 6.4).

Most of the students who took part in the survey reported that they had a strong entrepreneurial orientation and that the project had considerably contributed towards the development of said entrepreneurial attitude. In spite of proactiveness having obtained the lowest score in the individual assessment, it was at the same time considered as the most developed/enhanced attitude of the cross-curricular project. Similar results concerning students' satisfaction were obtained by Okudan and Rzasa (2006). This result has further strengthened our confidence in the efficiency of project-based activities for fostering the development of an entrepreneurial orientation.

6.6 Conclusions

In conclusion, PBL activities have become increasingly popular in recent years in the context of engineering programmes and are currently considered a more innovative methodology than traditional approaches. The authors have described the positive influence of a cross-curricular project in the development of individual entrepreneurial orientation among first-year engineering students within the context of the MdE entrepreneurial hub. The work carried out has led the authors to conclude that students felt encouraged when being more proactive and innovative, whereas their risk-taking attitude was not improved to the same extent. Taken together, these findings suggest that higher education institutions play an important role in the development of the entrepreneurial orientation of their students. In fact, the strength of our study lies in the positive influence of institutional initiatives in the education and training of future entrepreneurs.

Moreover, the authors have provided evidence of the fact that PBL activities contribute in terms of acquiring teamwork skills, time management, working under pressure and project management skills, in addition to acquiring a feeling of commitment towards their colleagues. The research into this area is still ongoing but seems likely to confirm previous hypothesis that this methodology positively influences the acquisition of skills among higher education students, though it requires an extra investment of time and effort. In addition, the authors found a potential area for improvement related to the link between the academic curriculum and its application in the cross-curricular project. These findings have important implications for pursuing alternative courses of action in order to find a meaningful link between theory and practice.

Although the authors believe their work could represent a starting point for further research in a similar framework, they acknowledge that it has some limitations. The most important limitation lies in the small size of the sample, which might not be representative of a larger population of engineering students. Future studies should concentrate on increasing the number of students involved in these activities, and searching for additional information related to the teaching and learning processes they experience. The authors consider this issue vital for future research, and therefore they hope to focus on enhancing the quality of the learning outcomes of this activity in future editions of our academic programmes. Finally, the importance of the role of the entire entrepreneurial ecosystem that enables students to enhance their potential as future entrepreneurs should be acknowledged

References

Blumenfeld, P. C., Soloway, E., Marx, R. W., Krajcik, J. S., Guzdial, M., & Palincsar, A. (1991). Motivating project-based learning: Sustaining the doing, supporting the learning. *Educational Psychologist*, *26*(3-4), 369–398.

Bolton, D. L., & Lane, M. D. (2012). Individual entrepreneurial orientation: Development of a measurement instrument. *Education + Training*, *54*(2/3), 219–233.

Botha, M. (2010). A project-based learning approach as a method of teaching entrepreneurship to a large group of undergraduate students in South Africa. *Education as Change*, *14*(2), 213–232.

Brush, C. (2012). Note on internal entrepreneurship education ecosystem. Babson Conference, May 2012.

Fernández-Laviada, A. (2014). *Global Entrepreneurship Monitor. Informe GEM España 2014.* Cantabria: Editorial de la Universidad de Cantabria.

Frank, M., Lavy, I., & Elata, D. (2003). Implementing the project-based learning approach in an academic engineering course. *International Journal of Technology and Design Education, 13*(3), 273–288.

Grant, M. M. (2002). Getting a grip on project-based learning: Theory, cases and recommendations. *Meridian: A Middle School Computer Technologies Journal, 5*(1), 83–86.

Hadim, H. A., & Esche, S. K. (2002). Enhancing the engineering curriculum through project-based learning. Frontiers in Education, 2002. FIE 2002. 32nd Annual.

Lehmann, M., Christensen, P., Du, X., & Thrane, M. (2008). Problem-oriented and project-based learning (POPBL) as an innovative learning strategy for sustainable development in engineering education. *European Journal of Engineering Education, 33*(3), 283–295.

Neck, H., Green, P., & Bush, C. (2014). *Teaching entrepreneurship: A practice-based approach.* Cheltenham: Edward Elgar.

Okudan, G. E., & Rzasa, S. E. (2006). A project-based approach to entrepreneurial leadership education. *Technovation, 26*(2), 195–210.

Thomas, J. W. (2000). *A review of research on project – Based learning.* California: The Autodesk Foundation. Downloaded from http://www.bie.org/index.php/site/RE/pbl_research/29.

Martina Luckanicova is a full-time professor responsible for entrepreneurship within EDEM Business School, developing an inclusive environment for entrepreneurs and enhancing entrepreneurship education system within Marina de Empresas. Before joining the university, she was a business developer manager at Spanish EdTech start-up Arloon. She holds PhD in Knowledge Management from the Technical University of Kosice (Slovakia), in addition to master's degree in Finance from Economic Faculty and Bachelor of Arts in European Business from Business School of University of Huddersfield (UK). She has published several research articles on Organizational Development, Knowledge Management and Economics.

Andrea Conchado holds a PhD in Industrial Engineering and works as a professor in EDEM, Business School and the Universidad Politécnica de Valencia. She has coauthored several research papers, books and book chapters in the areas of research methodology and applied statistics for social sciences, specifically the application of structural equation modelling to the assessment of the validity and reliability of measurement instruments. She has also collaborated as a researcher in several research projects funded by the European Commission in these research areas with partners from Latin America and the Balkan countries.

CHAPTER 7

Santander International Entrepreneurship Centre, University of Cantabria (Spain)

Federico Gutiérrez-Solana Salcedo, Inés Rueda Sampedro and Kerstin Maier

Abstract This case study aims at presenting the business model and the results of the Santander International Entrepreneurship Centre (CISE), an international reference Centre dedicated to fostering entrepreneurship and promoting the generation of start-ups. It provides a brief introduction into the Centre's context and stresses CISE's history and institutional set-up; this is followed by a presentation of its mission and vision on which its programmes and activities are based. It then highlights the Centre's distinctive comprehensive entrepreneurship and multi-stakeholder approach and provides insight into CISE's innovative training and support programmes. This case study concludes that it is possible to establish comprehensive strategies in support of an entrepreneurial culture through functional planning and coordination with own and other stakeholders' initiatives.

Keywords Business model · Spain · Start-ups · Entrepreneurship · Global · Stakeholders

---

F. Gutiérrez-Solana Salcedo (✉) · I. Rueda Sampedro · K. Maier
Santander International Entrepreneurship Centre (CISE), Santander, Spain
e-mail: director@cise.es; ines@cise.es; kerstin@cise.es

© The Author(s) 2017
G. Maas, P. Jones (eds.), *Entrepreneurship Centres*,
DOI 10.1007/978-3-319-47892-0_7

7.1 Introduction

This case study aims at presenting the business model and the results of the Santander International Entrepreneurship Centre (CISE), an international reference Centre dedicated to fostering entrepreneurship and promoting the generation of start-ups.

The case study starts with the presentation of the national context in which CISE is embedded in order to provide the reader with insight into the CISE's working environment. It then stresses the CISE's history and briefly explains its vision and mission since they constitute the basis upon which all programmes and activities are constructed, before emphasising on its distinctive comprehensive entrepreneurship approach that aims at fostering entrepreneurship in society from a global perspective, thereby contributing to the economic and social progress of its environment.

The CISE's innovative training programmes are then presented in detail, followed by the description of its growth and sustainability strategy as well as a brief description of its facilities. The chapter ends with a conclusion on the distinctive features of CISE considered to be contributing to the overall success of the Centre.

7.2 Background

The complex economic situation that Spain has undergone in recent years has had important negative consequences for society, the most crucial being the extremely high unemployment rate. One of the issues that the authors will analyse in more detail is the fact that entrepreneurship has received special attention lately for being considered one of the key elements to stimulate economic growth. Today's society is becoming more aware of the key role that innovation and entrepreneurship play in the development of a social and sustainable economy and there is an increasing number of organisations that have launched entrepreneurial initiatives aimed at supporting entrepreneurs in their various stages in recent years. Unfortunately, these activities often have not taken advantage of actors already working in this field causing inefficiencies and delays and not contributing in the best possible way to the development of an entrepreneurial ecosystem that fosters the development of a society able to address current problems.

Statistical data place Spain in terms of entrepreneurship and innovation behind other European countries. From one perspective, the Total early-stage Entrepreneurial Activity in Spain remains relatively low, 5.7 % in 2015 and 7 % in 2008 (Peña et al. 2016), half of the rate that it should have in accordance with its economic and productive model, the one corresponding to the innovative economies. Alternatively, the investment in R&D+I relative to GDP has been weakened considerably since the beginning of the crisis, from 1.37 in 2000 to 1.22 in 2014, in spite of its recognised importance in achieving private and public-sector competitiveness. In the last 15 years, productivity has stalled in Spain while it has continued to grow in other countries and the Global Competitiveness Index Report (Schwab 2015) shows that Spain lacks behind other countries with comparable economic capacity in terms of competitiveness (rank 33 on the global index). Among the indicators that constitute the competitiveness index, Spain fared lowest in government support for technological transfer (ranked 84th in the world context), private sector investment in R&D+I (ranked 59th), university-business investment in R&D+I (ranked 57th) and innovation (ranked 55th) showing that innovation is one of the weaknesses of the Spanish economy. According to these figures, the Spanish society faces a major challenge: maintain the current social welfare system and business sector through more competitiveness and innovation with a constrained availability of public and private funds to do so. It is therefore of crucial importance to boost the innovation capacity of private and public-sector stakeholders in order to increase productivity and economic social growth with the available financial resources. In this context, it is of particular importance to promote entrepreneurship, innovation and start-up creation. CISE does this through the promotion and support of an entrepreneurial and innovative culture with the ultimate goal of contributing to economic and social progress.

7.3 CISE's History

Given these premises and after analysing the situation of the various entities involved in the entrepreneurial environment in Cantabria, CISE was born in 2012 within the Cantabria International Campus of Excellence through an agreement of its promoter, the University of Cantabria (UC), the Regional Government of Cantabria and Santander Bank through its

Santander Universities Division, integrated as a Centre of the University of Cantabria under the structure of one of its foundations, UCEIF Foundation. The collaboration with Santander Bank arises from the longstanding relationship between the UC and Santander Bank established in 1996 as a pioneer project for the Santander University programme. Through Santander Universities, the bank has been able to establish more than 1,200 partnerships with universities and academic institutions around the world being the private entity that invests most in support of education worldwide. For its part, the Government of Cantabria supports several of the CISE programmes as part of its strategy of promoting entrepreneurship in the region. The UC is a public, young and modern institution whose main objective is to contribute to social progress through its commitment to teaching and scientific excellence. The more than forty years of experience and its focus on continuous improvement allowed the UC to be considered one of the top ten universities in the country in terms of scientific research production and quality. With the support of these three promoter entities, CISE shares the conviction that the Spanish society needs entrepreneurs with initiative, creativity, talent and enthusiasm, able to promote a more innovative society.

7.4 CISE's Vision, Mission and Structure

CISE's community comprises a wide network of local, national and international partners from the private, academic and public sector, more than 5,000 mainly Spanish entrepreneurs, and a workforce composed of a multidisciplinary and multicultural team of 17 people. CISE is convinced that in order to change society towards an entrepreneurial and innovative mindset, it is crucial to educate, train and support people with initiative, creativity, talent and enthusiasm in a highly inspiring collaborative entrepreneurial environment. CISE's mission is to create an improved society by encouraging its member's creative, entrepreneurial and innovative skills through a comprehensive approach that focuses not only on the support of entrepreneurs who want to set up their business but also on the education and training of people and the promotion of their entrepreneurial mindset as well as the creation of an inspiring network of talented people.

CISE seeks to be a reference centre in the international entrepreneurial ecosystem through its outstanding quality and results in terms of entrepreneurial research, awareness raising, education, training and the support of start-ups. The principles that guide all actions in CISE, both internally and externally, include social commitment, teamwork, quality, transparency, collaboration, innovation, lean methods, passion and knowledge. In line with these principles, CISE puts an emphasis on including smaller regions and cities in its activities in order to provide the local population with high-quality entrepreneurship programmes thereby promoting equality of opportunities on a national and international scale. In its collaboration with local, regional, national and international partners such as educational institutions, local development agencies and research institutions, it focuses on knowledge transfer and the exchange of best practices in order to facilitate skills and capacity development of entrepreneurship key stakeholders. CISE is constantly looking for new approaches and tendencies in entrepreneurship support and education and collaborates with leading entrepreneurship institutions, such as the Babson College, in order to ensure that their programmes respond in the best possible way to the needs and requirements of their partners and clients.

The above-stated values and principles are also reflected in the Centre's management structure and corporate culture. The conviction that CISE's community member's talent, knowledge and commitment are crucial to its success builds the core of its management structure. Its management processes focus on developing and promoting the engagement, capacities and knowledge of its community members through open and collaborative working methodologies and a horizontal management structure as well as an inspiring working environment. CISE selects its team members carefully according to the above-stated values and principles and actively communicates the Centre's focus on collaborative, multidisciplinary, project-based and client-focused work at all stages. It applies lean management approaches focused on its clients' needs for the design, testing, adaptation and implementation of its actions and seeks to constantly improve its programmes and support activities.

7.5 CISE's Comprehensive Working Approach

One of CISE's main objectives is the development of an entrepreneurial ecosystem at regional, national and international level that supports and promotes entrepreneurship from a holistic perspective. That is why CISE seeks to promote an entrepreneurial culture from a global perspective divided into four strategic working fields that are considered key to the development of an enhanced entrepreneurial and innovative society: entrepreneurial mindset development, entrepreneurial education, entrepreneurial support and knowledge transfer and entrepreneurial research.

CISE's comprehensive model not only covers all perceived key areas of entrepreneurship as specified in the preceding section, but also established a comprehensive network of partners, currently more than 200 public and private entities, in its attempt to cooperate with the whole range of entrepreneurship stakeholders such as national and regional governments, private companies, national and international organisations and experts, training organisations and investors, and of course pupils, students and entrepreneurs of all ages. It also counts on internationally recognised prestigious partners such as Babson College (USA) and one of the top Spanish Business Schools, Escuela de Organización Industrial (EOI) as well as international organisations such as the Organization of Ibero-American States and the Organization of Spanish University Rectors (CRUE), Universia and redEmprendia in order to ensure the quality of its programmes. CISE furthermore places special emphasis on interconnecting its initiatives and programmes in order to promote experience exchange and multidisciplinary among students, entrepreneurs, companies, experts, investors, government representatives and teachers with the ultimate goal of creating a high-impact entrepreneurial ecosystem.

7.6 CISE's Programmes

This section briefly explains the most significant data of the main programmes developed and coordinated by CISE. CISE is managing projects in four different strategic areas of its activity: research, entrepreneurial mindset, education and training and entrepreneurial support.

Entrepreneurial Mindset Development

Within this strategic working field CISE provides training aimed at the development of an entrepreneurial mindset with a focus on personal and transversal skills acquisition required not only for entrepreneurs but also for the society as a whole. CISE is currently working on further advancing and expanding its programmes in this working field on a national and international scale due to the demand of this kind of programmes by the involved stakeholders.

The e2 programme: student × entrepreneur is an innovative entrepreneurship training programme, complementary to the activities that universities develop regularly. e2 is a 6-month training programme that brings experienced entrepreneurs and students together to work on the creation and development of a business idea. It combines entrepreneurship training, multidisciplinary and multicultural teamwork, mentoring by successful entrepreneurs. The programme focuses on the first stage of the entrepreneurship cycle: from the creation of the business idea to the selection of a business model and the development of a value proposition. It not only generates knowledge on what it takes to generate exciting business opportunities and how to take ideas to market, but also fosters transversal skills such as the creation and development of multidisciplinary teams as well as intercultural communication skills. The first edition of the e2 programme started at the UC in 2012/2013. Since then 54 lead students, 203 fellow students and 60 business mentors have gone through the programme. The programme's success is shown by the following figures: the student and business mentors' overall satisfaction with the programme averages 4.6 on a 5.0 scale, 99 % of students completed the programme successfully and an average of 64 students were selected among 103 applications. The e2 students belong to 13 different faculties and both employers and students rate the multidisciplinary working group approach very highly, with 4.8 out of 5.0 points. Regarding intention to undertake and the development of an entrepreneurial culture, valued at 4.6 and 4.7 to 5.0. Furthermore, the programme contributed to the development of an entrepreneurial attitude of the participating students with a score of 4.7 out of the 5.0 scale. The programme is accredited by the UC as 'professional experience' and runs as 'optional study activities'.

Due to the success of e2 programme at the university level, the programme was launched in Vocational Training Institutes in an adapted version in 2013/2014 where the entrepreneurial training course is not only provided for the lead students and business mentors but also for the teachers and representatives of the Regional Education Ministry. In the two editions held so far, the programme trained 228 students and 17 teachers as well as 46 business mentors. The programme was also adapted to secondary education in 2013/2014 and currently runs under the name of 'STARTinnova' in collaboration with the media Vocento group and the support of the regional newspaper *Diario Montañes* in the autonomous region of Cantabria. In the 2016 edition, 29 secondary schools and companies participated in the programme and 480 pupils and 40 teachers were trained on entrepreneurial skills and capacities and a total of 178 entrepreneurial business projects were presented to a jury composed of local business executives, government representatives and education experts.

Once the project has been tested and analysed, it is on the basis of an European project with the aim to improve employability, providing students with transversal skills and interactive mindset, with the support of an international network of universities, companies and entrepreneurship experts.

Entrepreneurial Education

CISE's entrepreneurial education programmes are aimed at people with an entrepreneurial mindset and an entrepreneurial intention who want to improve their knowledge and skills regarding setting up a business.

The Master's Programme in Entrepreneurship, organised with the EOI, started in 2013/2014 at the UC and provides students regardless of their study degree with a transversal entrepreneurial training programme that runs simultaneously to the degree studies, thereby allowing students to acquire a double-degree and preparing them with a skills set that allows them to set up their own business or to create added value in an existing company or other fields. The programme focuses on enhancing students' entrepreneurial competences through real-life situations and hands-on practice in order to improve competencies like creativity, leadership, team management, negotiation and networking, and teaches students how to spot opportunities, generate ideas and put them into action.

The master's training sessions are held by successful entrepreneurs, executives from established companies, renowned academic and expert speakers on topics linked to the implementation of business ideas. Students can participate in a wide range of experiential sessions and conferences with regional entrepreneurs and are actively involved in an enriching network of entrepreneurs and innovation agents. The master's is accredited and usually takes three consecutive years of studying. It combines face-to-face sessions on Friday afternoons and Saturday mornings with online training and complementary entrepreneurial activities.

Start-Up Support and Knowledge Transfer

CISE provides support to entrepreneurs in order to help them set up their companies. People involved in one of the following projects typically possess entrepreneurial intention and require hands-on support on business creation with expert guidance and access to a network of entrepreneurs and investors.

YUZZ is a collaborative 7-month programme that aims at supporting young entrepreneurs, aged between 18 and 31, in the development and establishment of their technology-based business ideas through entrepreneurial training and support as well as expert advice and financial and non-financial awards, and the integration into a high-performance ecosystem where the projects can grow and turn into viable business models. The programme's main objective is to boost entrepreneurship through a collaborative ecosystem that promotes synergies and knowledge transfer among YUZZers, participants in the project. YUZZ values include teamwork, engagement, responsibility, creativity and innovation. It runs simultaneously at YUZZ centres all over Spain which are run by local organisations such as Universities or Local Development Agencies and is managed at a national and international scale by CISE. Santander Bank, through its Santander Universities Division, supports the programme financially and collaborates actively with it.

The programme's structure is as follows: the programme starts with a selection process of young entrepreneurs aged between 18 and 31 with an innovative technology-based business idea (YUZZers). Selection criteria include the creativeness and innovativeness of their business idea as well as their perceived motivation and engagement of accelerating their business project in a collaborative ecosystem. At the beginning of each edition, the local YUZZ centre launches a call of applicants and selects a maximum of 20 business ideas and 25 YUZZers. Following, the selected YUZZers are immersed in a guided acceleration process that combines training and expert advice with a set of complementary activities and awards for the best business ideas. The training is based on agile start-up methodologies and comprises a wide range of face-to-face and digital training and learning tools. The programme also includes a diverse set of networking activities aiming at promoting the interaction, communication and collaboration among YUZZers, thereby leveraging synergies and boosting knowledge transfer among the programmes´ stakeholders and projects.

Throughout the programme, YUZZers are encouraged to work on a series of deliverables that culminates with the development of a Business Plan that is included in the evaluation process of the award criteria. YUZZ awards include a 1-week-trip to Silicon Valley as well as financial awards and access to renowned acceleration programmes such as FinnTech and Ernst&Young Women Entrepreneurs. The success story of the programme is shown by the following programme results: the programme experienced an exponential growth from 2 YUZZ centres in 2008 to currently 48 centres in the 2016 edition. Moreover, 30 % of the participating projects resulted in business creation and participants' satisfaction clearly shows the overall success of the programme. YUZZ has been awarded in 2016 one of the three "Best European Practice Supporting Self-Employment" by the European Local Inclusion & Social Action Network (ELISAN) and the Regional Union of Municipalities of Attica (PEDA).

The entrepreneurship programme (DOCE) fosters innovative spin-offs. It is dedicated to doctoral students, researchers and professionals and seeks to encourage them into the creation of university spin-offs based on their research results through the fusion of scientific knowledge with business expertise. The programme's phases include training sessions on the generation of business ideas, selection of valid business models, as well as incubation and support during the business idea development. The programme also comprises competency and entrepreneurial skills development of its participants. DOCE is carried out over nine months and combines presence-based seminars, mentoring sessions and individual and collective work. In the pilot project initiated in 2015, 26 researchers developed their entrepreneurial competences and their project idea through this programme.

The Santander Advance programme is supported by Santander Bank and managed by CISE at a national scale, and its main objective is to foster the development and growth of Spanish small- and medium-sized enterprises (SMEs). It offers owners, managers and executives of SMEs from all over Spain the possibility to renew and further develop their knowledge on topics related to their businesses' key strategies through a wide range of activities, courses, workshops and seminars coordinated by CISE. These activities are part of Santander Bank's strategy to promote the development of SMEs while helping them to grow. The courses combine dynamic workshops held by well-known experts certified by the CISE partner business school (EOI), with debates on real-life experiences and time for interaction and networking, with the objective to provide executives with up-to-date information on the latest trends and groundbreaking tools to make them more capable of developing and leading successful positioning and expansion strategies in their businesses. The courses not only provide important information to SMEs but also generate a climate of interaction and experience exchange among the involved stakeholders and foster the relationship between SMEs and innovation and research environment of universities. The current edition comprises 13 courses and 14 seminars and involves

1,230 executives of SMEs from all over Spain. The current network of 'Santander Advance Alumni Club' includes more than 100 members who increasingly participate in other activities organised by CISE such as within the e2 programmes as business mentors as well as YUZZ experts, thereby contributing to the promotion of entrepreneurship in their regions and involving in activities outside their usual business environment.

Entrepreneurial Research

CISE focuses its research component on the analysis of previous and current research activities undergone in the field of entrepreneurship and its related topics on a national and international scale.

The Global Entrepreneurship Monitor (GEM) is the world's foremost study of entrepreneurship that aims at providing high-quality information on the entrepreneurial phenomena through the measurement of entrepreneurial activity, attitudes and aspirations of individuals. Within the framework of this global project, CISE leads and coordinates the Spanish GEM network which is formed by 130 researchers from the national academic and business world divided into 17 regional research teams. GEM Spain has the support of 90 institutions, universities and businesses. The project is sponsored by Santander Bank through Santander Universities as well as the Rafael del Pino Foundation.

The main aim of GEM is to measure the intent of the population in setting up their own business. Through a large number of indicators measured by GEM, the monitor seeks to analyse the kind of people that participate (or not) in entrepreneurial processes.

The data collected through the Adult Population Surveys measure entrepreneurial activity, attitudes and aspirations of individuals, and GEM evaluates the motivations that lead people towards entrepreneurial activity such as necessity, opportunity, income improvement or increased independence. GEM also analyses the effects of the environment through the National Survey of Experts, which measures the factors that affect national entrepreneurial activity in nine areas such as Finance, Government Policies, Training, among others. All this information is collected annually and summarised in a series of national and worldwide reports that include international, national and regional data and allow for comparison of date between countries, and in the case of Spain among regions. As with all the stakeholders of the CISE network,

GEM members are increasingly participating in other programmes and activities such as the YUZZ programme providing their expert knowledge to young entrepreneurs.

CISE promotes research projects in collaboration with research organisations and with the support of national and international university networks and foundations that aim at analysing and studying available data on the entrepreneurial phenomena in order to come up with insights into entrepreneurial activity and its impact on society. The Study on Corporate Entrepreneurship in Spain aims at developing a catalogue of best practices in corporate entrepreneurship and analyse the Spanish corporate entrepreneurial ecosystem.

The Spanish University Entrepreneurship Observatory analyses the development of students' entrepreneurial intention, studies the entrepreneurial profile of university students and analyses the entrepreneurial mindset of university students. The Entrepreneurial Activity and Productivity Study analyses the relationship between entrepreneurial activity and productivity of the Spanish autonomous communities and assesses the distinctive impact of different forms of entrepreneurship: high potential entrepreneurs, technological entrepreneurs and international entrepreneurs. The panel study of entrepreneurial dynamics analyses the entrepreneurial process over four years from the creation of a business idea until the set-up of a business.

7.7 Growth and Sustainability Strategy

Based on its mission to boost entrepreneurship, CISE constantly develops its programmes and activities further and responds to detected needs with the design and implementation of new programmes. It does so in collaboration with a wide range of collaborators who provide technical input as well as financial support. Its growth and financial strategy is based on the alliance with strategic partners who provide expert knowledge and the diversification of financial sources in order to ensure sustainability and quality of its programmes. After four years, the CISE budged has been multiplied by 20.

7.8 Installations

The unique working environment of CISE's installations is aimed at encouraging entrepreneurship, innovation and collaborative work. The Centre's philosophy becomes a reality in the co-working areas which include an open set of tiers inspired by an amphitheatre, a central square with a meeting and debate area and a flexible space dedicated to training (www.cise.es). The inspiring and dynamic character of the installations received recognition in national and international architecture journals (OfficeSnapshots, Espacios Interiores).

7.9 Conclusions and Implications

It is possible to establish comprehensive strategies in support of an entrepreneurial culture. It requires a clear vision, functional planning and coordination within the own and with other stakeholders' initiatives. CISE has proved in four years the way to do so and developed the entrepreneurial spirit of its environment in connection with national and international networks, coordinated projects and with the support of a large number of institutional partners guided by its principles of knowledge, confidence and collaboration.

References

Espacios Interiores. Retrieved from: http://www.espacios-interiores.com/revistas/digital/09/#/48/.
Office Snapshots. Retrieved from: https://officesnapshots.com/2015/07/08/the-santander-international-entrepreneurship-center/.
Peña, I., Guerrero, M., & González-Pernía, J. L. (2016). *Informe GEM España 2015*. ISSN: 1695-9302. Spain.
Schwab, K. (2015). *The global competitiveness report 2015–2016*. ISBN-13: 978-92-95044-99-9. Geneva.

Federico Gutiérrez-Solana Salcedo has a Master's in Civil Engineering (UPM, 1975) and received his doctorate in 1981 with Extraordinary Prize of the Polytechnic University of Madrid. He has been Research Associate at Carnegie-Mellon University (1981–1983); professor since 1984 and professor since 1989 at the University of Cantabria; Visiting professor at Carnegie-Mellon, Tufts (Boston) and Paris-XI (Orsay) Universities. He was honoured for his research and knowledge transfer achievements by the European Conference of Fracture, the Social Council of the University of Cantabria and the Red FUE. He received the Medal of Honour of the Spanish Fracture Group, the Medal of Professional Merit of the School of Civil Engineering, C. and P. and the Medal of Honor of the National Civil Engineering College. He was Director of the Civil Engineering Department of the University of Cantabria (1987–1995), Vice Chancellor for Faculty and Planning (1997–2002) and Rector (2002–2012). He was also Vice

President of the Spanish Conference of University Deans CRUE (2007–2009) and President (2009–2011). He was Vice President of Universia (2009–2011), Chairman of the Academic Committee of the II Meeting of Universia of Guadalajara (Mexico, 2010) and Chairman of the Technical Secretariat of the Third Meeting of Rio de Janeiro (2014). Since 2012, Federico leads Santander International Entrepreneurship Centre, a centre created with the support of Banco Santander, the University of Cantabria and the Government of Cantabria, dedicated to the promotion and support of entrepreneurship.

Inés Rueda Sampedro has an MSc in Business Administration (University of Cantabria, 2009), MBA (University of Cantabria, 2010) and is currently a PhD candidate in the Department of Business Administration at the University of Cantabria. Her doctoral thesis focuses on the impact of education on students' entrepreneurial intention. She is a team member of the Global Entrepreneurship Monitor since 2011 and currently works as Technical Project Manager at Santander International Entrepreneurship Centre (CISE), where he is responsible for the research area. Her functions at CISE include the coordination of the Network of Regional Teams that makes up GEM in Spain.

Kerstin Maier obtained an MSc in Business Administration (University of Augsburg, 2004) and MA in International Project Planning and Management (UNED, 2010). She has worked as project manager and business consultant for international organisations and multinational companies in the interface between the private and public sector in the areas of foreign trade, capacity building and entrepreneurship (UN WOMEN, SIEMENS, SPRIM; AHK, GIZ, 2004–2014). She is currently the Deputy Assistant to the Director at Santander International Entrepreneurship Center (2015–present).

CHAPTER 8

The Hunter Centre for Entrepreneurship and Innovation (Canada)

Simon Raby

Abstract This chapter presents a case study on the Hunter Centre for Entrepreneurship and Innovation operating in North America. The case study was formed through a formal interview with the Director of the Centre, a range of informal conversations with academic and support staff of the Centre and those within the entrepreneurial ecosystem, over a period of *six* months, with archival documentation studied to corroborate and substantiate the findings. As their annual report states, the Centre has focused on developing 'support' across the entrepreneurial and student communities. Next is to 'establish' and then 'sustain' over the next *ten* years (HCEI, Engaging a new generation of entrepreneurial thinkers, Hunter Centre for Entrepreneurship and Innovation, 2014–2015 Annual Report, 2015). To achieve this, one particular aspect is the location of the Centre, which is currently being debated. No decision has yet been made; however, as the activities of the Centre cascade further across faculty, it was commented that it might make sense for the Centre to report to central faculty. How to measure success is another area that, to date, has not been fully crystallised.

S. Raby (✉)
Centre for Employment, Competitiveness and Growth, Kent Business School, University of Kent, Kent, UK
e-mail: simon.raby@haskayne.ucalgary.ca

Keywords Support · Establish · Sustain · Entrepreneurship · HEIs · Canada

8.1 Introduction

This chapter presents a case study on the Hunter Centre for Entrepreneurship and Innovation (HCEI) at the University of Calgary in North America. The case study was formed through a formal interview with the Director of the Centre, a range of informal conversations with academic and support staff of the Centre and those within the entrepreneurial ecosystem, over a period of six months, with archival documentation studied to corroborate and substantiate the findings. The case study will be structured as follows:

- Situating the Centre within its broader context: Here, the broader contextual features of the environment within which the Centre performs its duties is considered.
- Understanding the Centre: The evolution of the Centre, its achievements and its challenges is discussed in this category.
- Concluding remarks and implications: Finally, the case reflects on the lessons the Centre and its staff have learnt.

8.2 Situating the Centre within Its Broader Context

The HCEI operates as part of the business school faculty on the main campus of the University of Calgary. The University of Calgary started life as the Calgary branch of the University of Alberta in 1945, gaining full autonomy in 1966. The University is in its 50th anniversary year and was recently ranked 1st in Canada and North America and 18th internationally in the '150 under 50' *Times Higher Education* global rankings (THE 2016). The University is deemed to be one of the top research-intensive universities in Canada, being a member of the select 'U15' *Group of Canadian Research Universities* (www.u15.ca) and ranking 6th in the Top 50 Canadian Research Institutions based on income (www.researchinfosource.com). The University is second largest by revenue and endowment within the province of Alberta and boasts some 14 faculties and more than 85 research institutes and centres.

The University's motto *Mo shùile togam suas*, which translated from Gaelic means *I will lift up my eyes*, featured prominently in the latest strategic vision launched in 2011 (University of Calgary 2011). This 'Eyes High' strategy set an ambitious target for the University to become by 2016 one of "Canada's top five research Universities, grounded in innovative learning and teaching and fully integrated with the community of Calgary". This strategy has been overseen by the current President and Vice Chancellor Elizabeth Cannon, a Canadian Geomatics Engineer by trade. The University's main campus occupies 530 acres of land northwest of Calgary city, with a separate Health Sciences campus, along with a downtown campus that was inaugurated in 2010.

The Haskayne School of Business: 'Where Leaders Learn to Lead'
The University's school of business started life in 1967 as a Faculty of Management and has roots in energy and real estate. By 1986, the business school had moved into its own purpose-built facility named after the late Ralph Scurfield, a respected home builder and land developer, who donated considerable funds to build the school. The school itself is named after Richard F. Haskayne, a chartered accountant born and raised in Alberta and former Chairman of the board of TransCanada Corporation, who donated a parcel of land and $16 million to the School in 2002, representing the largest charitable donation in the history of the University. The school now has over 4,400 full-time and part-time students, enrolled in bachelor's, master's, doctorate and executive education, with 22,000 alumni in more than 80 countries worldwide. The school was the second and now one of only 19 Canadian business schools to gain accreditation to the Association to Advance Collegiate Schools of Business (AACSB) in 1985, with AACSB seen as a hallmark of excellence, being earned by less than 5% of business schools globally. The school is internationally recognised for its Global Energy Executive MBA and by the performance of its students at the Inter-Collegiate Business Competition hosted annually by Queen's University in Ontario.

Entrepreneurship is clearly visible as one of three pillars of the vision for Haskayne School of Business "to be an internationally recognized Centre of excellence for graduate and undergraduate business education, research, and community engagement. We will emphasize those distinct elements that define Calgary and Alberta: ethical leadership, entrepreneurship, and energy" (Haskayne School of Business, 2016). Entrepreneurship has held popular parlance at the school since its inception, formally a central part of the early MBA.

The area of entrepreneurship is championed by the current Dean of the business school. As an Associate Professor in Strategy and Global Management, the Dean has contributed to the field of management by developing constructs of cognitive resilience, entrepreneurial thinking and new understanding on the strategic response that firms take to disruptive innovation. Prior to entering academia, the Dean was CEO of two major real estate development companies and a leading local engineering consulting practice.

Inspired by the Eyes High strategy, the business school invested in a five-year philanthropic campaign, 'Where Leaders Learn to Lead'. Launched in 2011, the target was to raise $50 million in five years, a figure surpassed by end of 2015. To date, an impressive $53 million has been raised from more than 1,700 donors. Five notable donors (HCEI 2013), gifting a combined $8 million, founded the HCEI in their shared desire to embed entrepreneurial thinking to the curriculum. HCEI is one of nine Centres at the school, with Centres exploring the latest thinking in leadership, real estate, sustainability, finance, accounting, informatics, risk, supply chain and tourism.

Region in Which the University Operates

Calgary's potential was unlocked by the construction of a station for the Canadian Pacific Railway in 1883. From then onwards, pioneers were encouraged to Alberta by the offer of free land (Homestead Congress 2010) and agriculture soon became a key component of the economy. Much of the provinces' subsequent development occurred from the rich reserves of oil, gas and lumber. The economy of today is diverse and cosmopolitan, with a thriving cultural sector. Together, these industrial developments have driven economic and societal growth, with the city now boasting a population of 1.35 million (660 news 2014).

Conditions are generally favourable for residents of Calgary and surrounding neighbourhoods. Indeed, the business school has even labelled this the 'Calgary advantage' within their promotional literature, highlighting the national head office concentration (Roach 2010), quality of living, the pleasant weather and the city reputation as a cultural hub. Whilst property prices have increased, the city is still seen as an affordable option when compared to other major cities of Vancouver in the West and Toronto in the East (CREA 2016). The province is presently governed by the National Democratic Party, a left-wing party that took power from the long-standing Conservative Government in 2015.

The vast majority of all organisations across Alberta are small, having between 1 and 99 employees (98.2 %). Four out of every five people in the working population are employed by a small firm, and over 90 % of all employees work for small- and medium-sized enterprises (SMEs) (Statistics Canada 2013). Whilst interesting at a macro level, this type of data does not provide the micro-level insights that are required to build evidence-based policy and practice. Global Entrepreneurship Monitor research reveals that Alberta boasts the highest rate of 'early stage entrepreneurship',[i] reflecting the prevalence of start-up activities in Calgary (Toneguzzi 2015), with Canada second only to the USA in levels of entrepreneurial activity (CBC news 2015).

The entrepreneurial ecosystem is supported by government through funded incubators (e.g. Innovate Calgary) and privately funded incubators that tend to focus on particular sectors or types of business (e.g. District Ventures and Zone Startups). 'Startup Calgary' was launched in 2012 and is a branch of the national organisation Startup Canada that was founded by entrepreneurs 'to build an environment for entrepreneurship'. The financial sector is also ever present with the Alberta treasury Branch (ATB) Finance and the Business Development Bank of Canada (BDC) offering entrepreneurial financing products. Both ATB (through their quarterly 'Business Beat' feature) and BDC release a range of industry insight reports on business across the province.

8.3 The Hunter Centre for Entrepreneurship and Innovation

Entrepreneurial Thinking: The Importance of a Transcending Niche

HCEI was founded in 2013, made possible by a $8 million in endowments of local entrepreneurs, an investment that took "three to four years of relationship building to land". The Centre has now generated a total revenue since its inception of $9.8 million of gifts, comprised of an endowment (39 %) and operating funds (61 %). Expenditure for the 2014/2015 financial year was $736,978. The Centre has set an ambitious target to raise $25 million by 2025. The promise of embedding entrepreneurial thinking into the student curriculum reportedly convinced the donor group to get on board, with the Centre aiming to transform the teaching of entrepreneurship. Because the gift was originally given to the business school, the Centre is located in the business school on the main University campus.

The vision of the Centre is "to build a world class Centre of excellence in entrepreneurial thinking" (HCEI, 2015). The Centre is presently locally focused, in the view that "local success breeds provincial and national success". The focus on a niche in entrepreneurial thinking has helped the Centre to broaden its impact and reach and develop interdisciplinary cross-campus support: "it takes us away from purely startups and commercialization... and reduces the conflict... to a position where we have cross campus support". The Centre has five strategic pillars that seek to enable entrepreneurship and innovation through

- teaching curriculum for undergraduate and postgraduate students (e.g. 'entrepreneurial thinking')
- student development (e.g. co-curriculum, competitions)
- research agenda/activities (e.g. strategic research grants initiative)
- community outreach (e.g. entrepreneur speaker series)
- continuous improvement/strategic development (e.g. building the team, continued fundraising).

Fitting in: The Crucial Role of a Central Faculty Champion

The activities of the Centre, whilst initially for business school students only, have propagated across campus through a relationship between the Director of the HCEI and central faculty: "We [the Director of HCEI and the Associate Vice President for Research (AVPR)] identified a unique opportunity for entrepreneurship to become part of the portfolio [of faculty programs]". The Centre Director continues: "He [the AVPR] elevated the importance of entrepreneurship at a central faculty level. Entrepreneurship and innovation wasn't expressed explicitly as part of the university's plan, but it is intended that this will feature in the next iteration".

The way to create student learning in entrepreneurship was debated prior to launching the Centre in a desire to open up opportunities across campus. However, there were some initial challenges, not least the fees that students have to pay to join the MBA programme:

> In my first week of work... he [the AVPR] contacted me and said 'it is time!' We negotiated with the Dean of the School of Business for five places on the MBA for non-MBA students. The view was that other students would take a different view of entrepreneurship and innovation, and would add value to

business school students. The fees and pre-requisites were waved. This was the beginning of a cross campus collaboration/profile for entrepreneurship.

Whilst in its early stages, the inclusion of entrepreneurship is being witnessed as a topic of conversation within the current University strategic development process. It appears that this gave birth to a central Academic Committee for Entrepreneurship and Innovation chaired by the AVPR: "he [AVPR] played a pivotal role. We could do this for everyone! Be brave and bold, think big!"

Building a Vision: The Importance of Foresight and Insight

The current Director of HCEI is a former competitive athlete (swimming), a Political Sciences graduate, with an MBA from the University of British Columbia, who played a key role in the MBA programme at the University of Toronto. In taking the role as Director of HCEI, she professed to know little about Centres of Entrepreneurship, but held knowledge of the unique ways that business schools and universities worked: "I knew nothing about how to run an Entrepreneurship Centre…I knew how to navigate in the context of a business school and how to work with central faculty, the structures, rules and curriculum development. But, when it came to knowing what entrepreneurial thinkers and leaders needed; I was like a deer in headlights!"

A key event that occurred in the history of developing the strategy for HCEI involved meeting her counterpart at another Calgary-based institution. Whilst both shared similar challenges, her alter ego came from industry and they supported each other in the early days of developing their respective Centres: "[I was asking] what did an Entrepreneurship Centre need to do or be? I met my counterpart from Mount Royal. We couldn't be more different. I have experience of top tier schools and he is an entrepreneur. We both faced similar challenges [he was also setting up an Entrepreneurship Centre]. He raised the GCEC [Global Consortium of Entrepreneurship Centers] conference in Kansas and said let's go! So we did!"

At time of interview, the Director of HCEI referred to a book entitled *Entrepreneurship Programs and the Modern University* by Morris et al. (2013) and how this text, and in particular the presentation delivered by Michael Morris at the annual conference for the GCEC, had provided an important roadmap for the Centre: "We were 'spinning our wheels' for a while trying to work out our vision and the best model. It became clear that the business school was the natural Centre of research and teaching... and that entrepreneurship had been narrowly defined in terms of startup and new venture creation".

Aligned to the strategic pillars outlined earlier, the current objectives of the Centre are to develop

- Teaching curriculum: a comprehensive student experience programme that is experiential academically and includes co-curriculum programming at the undergraduate and postgraduate levels.
- Research agenda/activities: recruiting a senior research chair and developing a foundation for a robust research programme.
- Community outreach: developing approaches to better engage industry with the Centre via mutually value-added experiences around the theme of entrepreneurship.
- Continuous improvement/strategic development: fundraising to reach a target of $25 million and building a sustainable financial model for the Centre.

Developing a Presence: Investing in a Team of Teaching and Support Staff

Aside to the central faculty advisory committee, the Centre also has an academic faculty committee, upon which research-active staff from across the business school preside, and a sponsor committee that is chaired by one of the founding donors. The Centre has one direct member of faculty staff who holds a teaching professorship in entrepreneurial thinking. This position, with support from the Foundation of the Royal Bank of Canada (RBC), has played a central role in helping the Centre to promote and embed entrepreneurial thinking to academic programmes across the University. The post is directly responsible for "developing the entrepreneurial thinking curriculum and expanding Haskayne's teaching and learning to cross-campus entrepreneurship education" (Haskayne School of Business 2015). In addition to the Director and the teaching professorship roles, the Centre has three full-time support staff, including an Associate Director, a Community

Engagement Manager and an administrative assistant, and a part-time summer internship position.

Entrepreneurial Thinking Enables Cross Faculty Teaching Delivery

> **Fast Pitch 2016 winner**
> Cups2Go identified that customers attending movie theatres often struggle when attempting to carry food and beverages to seats from concessions. Cups2Go has designed a sleek, innovative, paper–thin carry design that enhances the end consumer's movie theatre experience by allowing for easy transportation of their food and drink.

Being part of the business school, a named faculty on campus, the Centre is believed well positioned to take a leadership role in the development of foundation courses in entrepreneurship. The 'Entrepreneurial Thinking' course is available to bachelor of commerce students and was formally launched in September 2014. The course aims to help students "develop an entrepreneurial mindset by brainstorming possibilities, solving problems, and ultimately creating their own new venture concept aimed at capturing a market opportunity" (HCEI 2015). In 2015/2016, the course attracted 650 undergraduates and 150 graduates from across campus. Students form into teams of five, each identifying an opportunity, conducting relevant research into the market potential and developing a new venture concept. The course culminates with the 'Fast Pitch' competition which, like the teaching professorship, is supported by RBC. Twelve teams pitch their feasibility assessments to a panel of judges made up of entrepreneurs, RBC investment staff and university teaching faculty. Prizes are considerable, with first prize being $100,000 in cash and in-kind prizes to kick-start the winning team's business idea.

In partnership with Innovate Calgary, the Centre leads a similar competition for technology start-ups in the energy sector ('The Energy New Venture Competition') and a range of other extracurricular student development and training (e.g. pitch coaching, incubator programmes and clinics). Beyond these local activities, the Centre annually leverages its profile through Global Entrepreneurship Week, hosting a range of events, delivering live case studies, inviting entrepreneurs to share their stories and releasing awards to celebrate student achievement.

Entrepreneurship Research: Early Stage Initiatives Attract Interest

The Centre is focused on developing a robust research programme on entrepreneurship and innovation and, as the Director comments, is seeking to develop a niche in entrepreneurial thinking: "...through the uniqueness of entrepreneurial thinking we can deliver something that doesn't currently exist [across Canada]...we have been successful across campus because we have used entrepreneurial thinking [to transcend academic boundaries]".

Of noteworthy importance is the publication of a book by the current Dean of the business school on entrepreneurial thinking, which was published because he was: "...concerned that businesses in general, and business leaders in particular, have lost touch with the all-important entrepreneurial spirit that drove growth and prosperity in the past".

However, the Centre has not been unchallenged in its broader research aspirations. Securing academic leadership has been no easy task, and this has visibly slowed the development of its research profile. The Centre's research activities are currently focused on encouraging staff from other discipline areas to become involved with its work through a 'strategic research grants initiative'. This initiative provides funds of up to $10,000 to staff of the business school to progress a piece of original research in the area of entrepreneurship and innovation. Six projects were supported in 2014/2015 at a total cost of $18,000.

Strategic Research Initiative – Case
Liena Kano, Assistant Professor in Strategy and Global Management, received $4,000 to conduct a research project addressing entrepreneurial family business governance from a new theoretical perspective. The study will offer actionable managerial insights for entrepreneurs on family firms' successful internationalization (and consequent longevity and survival).

Most recently, a partnership has been created between HCEI and a Research Centre in the UK – The Centre for Employment, Competitiveness and Growth (ECG), based at the University of Kent. Enabled through the Leverhulme Trust (A UK research council), HCEI is hosting a Visiting Professor from ECG to deliver a novel programme of research and community engagement on the practices that define sustainable growth amongst SMEs. Focused initially on the province of Alberta, it is expected that this work will provide considerable insights for academic, business and policy-making communities, and will enable the Centre, and the school more broadly, to build profile and gain legitimacy in the local/provincial market. The work aligns directly with the goals of the Centre, and the desire to develop programmes that have implications for organisations across the whole business continuum, from start-up through succession.

Awards Are Made to Recognise the Progress Achieved

The progress that the Centre has made in its first three years has not gone unnoticed. The Centre is a year ahead of its operational target, having embedded entrepreneurial thinking into curriculum across campus. It is not surprising that in late 2015 the Centre was the first Canadian recipient to be recognised by GCEC in the 'Emerging Entrepreneurship Center' category. Most recently, the Centre's Director has been recognised by the Calgary Herald's annual publication *Compelling Calgarians* (Calgary Herald 2016) which identifies 'individuals making their mark on our city'.

Scaling and Sustainability: The Challenges That Lie Ahead

In exploring the challenges that lie ahead for the Centre, six key themes emerged (see Table 8.1). During the interview, the Director's top challenges included *building a sustainable business model* and *scaling up*. To achieve a sustainable business model, the Centre needs to diversify its revenue streams. In addition to philanthropic donations, the Director is keen to secure income via funding and equity investment opportunities (i.e. by taking shares in businesses), generating commercial income (e.g. executive education and continuing education), creating a certified programme that can be embedded to existing provision and delivering programmes for community, not just the university. The Director was also adamant that the Centre needs to understand how it can scale its

Table 8.1 Key challenges experienced by a growing Entrepreneurship Centre

Key challenges experienced	Key questions these challenges raise
Creating a sustainable business model	How to build the Centre and develop revenue streams beyond philanthropic donations?
Scaling the teaching offer	How to deliver experiential programmes for 50,000 students and move beyond traditional modes of delivery?
Developing curriculum content	How to move beyond current faculty working in the area of entrepreneurship and innovation?
Being seen as a leader for research in entrepreneurship and innovation	How to identify and secure academic research leadership within the Centre? The current Director believes they do not hold legitimacy with academic-/research-focused faculty.
Effectively managing the relationship with University's commercialisation function	What type of relationship should the Centre have with the externalised commercialisation function beyond a transactional subcontractor?
Building a matching process for entrepreneur mentors and students	How to develop a matching process that is effective and not time intensive?

activities to move from 800 students to 50,000. Through our conversation it became clear that the Centre is dreaming big, keeping its 'eyes high' and is aware of the developments that need to take place to ensure the Centre achieves even more success in the future.

8.4 Conclusions

As their annual report states, the Centre has focused on developing 'support' across the entrepreneurial and student communities. Next is to 'establish' and then 'sustain' over the next ten years (HCEI 2015). To achieve this, the Centre is focused on resolving the challenges outlined earlier, as well as tackling other key issues head on. One particular aspect is the location of the Centre, which is currently being debated. No decision has yet been made; however, as the activities of the Centre cascade further across faculty, it was commented that it might make sense for the Centre to report to central faculty. How to measure success is another area that, to date, has not been fully crystallised. The Director spoke in aspirational terms in regard to measurement and that the Centre, if it is to prove that its focus on entrepreneurial thinking is right, will need to find ways to measure and track the change in mindset that occurs across the student body in response to programming. Finally, the Director recognises their limitations and that the research programme will only develop once there is academic leadership. At the time of writing this case study, the business school had recruited two new dedicated research-focused posts in entrepreneurship, although it remains to be seen if these posts will have a demonstrable impact on the research ambitions of the Centre.

NOTE

i. Defined as 'those people actively preparing new ventures and those with businesses under three-and-a-half years old'.

REFERENCES

660 News. (2014). Calgary leads Canada in terms of population growth: some question whether we can afford it, February 26, 2014. Downloaded from: http://www.660news.com/2014/02/26/calgary-leads-canada-in-terms-of-population-growth-some-question-whether-we-can-afford-it/.

Calgary Herald (2016). Compelling Calgarians: 20 people you'll want to watch in 2016, Downloaded from: www.calgaryherald.com.

CBC News. (2015). Entrepreneurship in Canada ranks 2nd in world, report says, May 29th 2015, Downloaded from: www.cbc.ca/news/business.

CREA, (2016), Canadian home sales decline further in June, Monthly Stats - National Statistics.

Haskayne School of Business. (2015). RBC Foundation invests $750,000 in entrepreneurship education, February 2015, Downloaded from: www.ucalgary.ca/utoday/.

Haskayne School of Business. (2016). Welcome to Haskayne, University of Calgary. Downloaded from: https://haskayne.ucalgary.ca/news/welcome-haskayne.

HCEI. (2013). Hunter Centre for Entrepreneurship and Innovation, Haskayne School of Business Youtube Channel, Published online 2 May 2013.

HCEI. (2015). Engaging a new generation of entrepreneurial thinkers, Hunter Centre for Entrepreneurship and Innovation, 2014–2015 Annual Report, Haskayne School of Business, University of Calgary, Canada.

Homestead Congress. (2010). The Canadian Homestead Act, 17 December 2010, Downloaded from: http://homesteadcongress.blogspot.ca/2010/12/canadian-homestead-act.html.

Morris, M. H., Kuratko, D. F., & Cornwall, J. R. (2013). Entrepreneurship Programs and the Modern University, Edward Elgar Publishing. ISBN 978-1-78254-462-3.

Roach, R. (2010). *State of the West: Western Canadian demographic and economic trends.* The West in Canada research Series, Going for Gold Project, Canada West Foundation, Calgary, Alberta.

Statistics Canada. (2013). Key Small Business Statistics, Small Business Branch, Industry Canada. Downloaded from: www.ic.gc.ca.

THE. (2016). 150 best young universities in the world, Times Higher Education University Rankings, Downloaded from: www.timeshighereducation.com/news.

Toneguzzi, M. (2015). Alberta's rate of entrepreneurship best in Canada, Downloaded from: www.calgaryherald.com

University of Calgary. (2011). Eyes high vision and strategy, Alberta, Canada. Downloaded from: http://ucalgary.ca/research.

Simon Raby is Visiting Professor of the Hunter Centre for Entrepreneurship and Innovation at the University of Calgary's Haskayne School of Business, a founding member of the Centre for Employment, Competitiveness at the University of Kent's Business School and a Director of Business Improvement and Growth (BIG) Associates Ltd, a university spinout that supports business schools in their quest to research and work with entrepreneurs and small- and medium-sized enterprises (SMEs) in their regions. Simon helped to build a multidisciplinary international applied research programme 'Promoting Sustainable Performance' to challenge the way SMEs achieve growth and has developed leadership tools and programmes so that SMEs can apply this new thinking. Simon serves on the Board of the Institute for Small Business and Entrepreneurship (ISBE), is educated to doctoral level and is an accredited and practising coach and facilitator. Simon is on the editorial board of the *International Journal of Entrepreneurial Behavior and Research* (IJEBR); a guest editor for the online journal of the Association for Management Education and Development (AMED) Organisations and People; and continues to write for academic, business and policy audiences on topics central to SME's growth and success.

CHAPTER 9

Centre for Entrepreneurship and Small Enterprises Development, University of Cape Coast (Ghana)

Rosemond Boohene and Daniel Agyapong

Abstract The Centre for Entrepreneurship and Small Enterprise Development (CESED) grows and supports entrepreneurial thinking and practice through education, training and research. These objectives are achieved through three interrelated activities: entrepreneurship education, research and publications, and business incubation. CESED has also established linkages with over fifty companies in the private sector where young entrepreneurs go through mentoring and coaching. Furthermore, the Centre adopts a multidisciplinary approach to its projects' implementation bringing together people from business, agribusiness, computer and natural sciences and other disciplines.

R. Boohene (✉)
Centre for Entrepreneurship and Small Enterprise Development, School of Business, University of Cape Coast, Cape Coast, Ghana
e-mail: rboohene@ucc.edu.gh

D. Agyapong
Department of Marketing and Supply Chain Management, School of Business, University of Cape Coast, Cape Coast, Ghana
e-mail: dagyapong@ucc.edu.gh

© The Author(s) 2017
G. Maas, P. Jones (eds.), *Entrepreneurship Centres*,
DOI 10.1007/978-3-319-47892-0_9

Keywords Education · Research · Business incubation · Small Enterprises · Entrepreneurship

9.1 INTRODUCTION

The Centre for Entrepreneurship and Small Enterprise Development (CESED) grows and supports entrepreneurial thinking and practice through education, training and research. These objectives are achieved through three interrelated activities: entrepreneurship education, research and publications, and business incubation. The Centre has a network of about 60 consultants, mainly in Ghana, who help with the nurturing and encouraging business ideas from students and would-be entrepreneurs. The Centre also brings on board expertise from experienced academics, consultants, corporate executives and other experts from Africa and Europe who are committed to achieving the main objectives of consulting, research, teaching and business incubation in order to re-engineer the small- and medium-sized enterprises (SMEs) sector in Ghana and to also link them to foreign partners. This write up examines and catalogues the activities of the Centre with the aim of explaining the role it plays in developing and nurturing the entrepreneurial skills and mindsets of the youth in Ghana.

9.2 THE UNIVERSITY OF CAPE COAST

The University of Cape Coast (UCC) was established on 15 December 1962 as a University College and placed in a special relationship with the University of Ghana. On 1st October 1971, the university attained the status of a full independent University with the authority to confer its own degrees, diplomas and certificates by an Act of Parliament – the University of Cape Coast Act 1971 (Act 390) and subsequently the University of Cape Coat Law 1992 (PNDC Law 278).

The UCC was established out of the need for highly qualified and skilled manpower in the teaching and development of the nation's human capital. Thus, it was established to train graduate teachers for senior high schools; a mission that the two Universities existing at the time were ill-equipped to fulfil. The University has since its establishment added to its functions programmes of study such as educational planning and administration; accounting, management studies and human resource management; nursing and medicine; environmental science, governance, agriculture and law and, recently, entrepreneurship. It is, therefore, playing a unique and vital role in the nation's efforts at strengthening its educational sector. These increases in programmes have caused an increase in student intake putting pressure on the existing accommodation facilities. As part of its entrepreneurial initiative, the University introduced Distance Education about a decade ago. It currently has over 42,000 distance education students in about 73 study centres around the country.

The University is an equal opportunity institution that is uniquely placed to provide quality education through the provision of comprehensive, liberal and professional programmes that challenge learners to be creative, innovative and morally responsible citizens. Through distance learning, it also extends expertise and facilities to train professionals for the education enterprise and business by employing modern technologies. The University constantly seeks alternative ways to respond to changing needs (University of Cape Coast Strategic Plan, 2015). The institution continues to expand its existing highly qualified faculty and administrative staff, offering a conducive environment that motivates them to position the University to respond effectively to the development needs of a changing world. This is the UCC's mission, which it pursues through its colleges, faculties and schools, institutes and centres – the School of Business being one of such Schools.

The School of Business (formerly Department of Business Studies), established in the 2004/2005 academic year, is one of the fourteen faculties in the University. The School has through the University's mission carved out a niche to be one of the leading providers of entrepreneurship education in Ghana. This emphasis by the School was borne out of the need to develop students who will become entrepreneurial in their thinking and also encourage those who may want to set up their own business in the future. As a first step, the School developed strategic partnerships with the Ghana National Chamber of Commerce and Industry, corporate bodies, consulting firms and industry experts in Ghana and Germany through the inter-university partnership programmes sponsored by the German government through the German Federal Ministry of Economic Cooperation and Development (BMZ) and the German Academic Exchange Service (DAAD) and implemented together with Bonn-Rhein-Sieg University of Applied Sciences (BRSU) in Germany. Consequently, a proposal was developed to set up the Centre for Entrepreneurship and Small Enterprise Development (CESED).

9.3 Centre for Entrepreneurship and Small Enterprise Development

The world economic crisis has had a dramatic impact on the challenges facing young people seeking jobs. Between 2008 and 2012, according to the Global Employment Trend Report (2014) published by the International Labour Organisation, the youth unemployment rate has seen the largest annual increase on record, reversing the pre-crisis trend on declining youth unemployment rates since 2002 and rising to 13% in 2012. The situation in Ghana is not different. According to a World Bank Report released in the early 2016, Ghana has a youth employment rate of 48%. Furthermore, figures from the Institute of Statistical Social and Economic Research indicate that there are currently over 200,000 unemployed graduates in Ghana (ISSER, 2015). The number was expected to increase to 271,000 due to the number of students graduating from both private and public tertiary institutions.

The attention to youth employment and the need to address entrepreneurship education, therefore, are present in coherent cross-sectorial strategies and integrated frameworks that connect Ghana's poverty reduction strategy, the Decent Work Agenda (ILO, 2007) and the National Youth Policy (Ministry of Youth and Sports, 2010) at the national and local levels. Entrepreneurial development, among other factors, propels and accelerates socio-economic development. However, its development is limited to a small section of the youth. Government realises the need to mainstream entrepreneurial development into school curricula to give it the necessary impetus. Such entrepreneurial development will be achieved through the integration of entrepreneurial skills into youth development activities, facilitation of access to credit for the youth, creation of corps of young entrepreneurs to serve as role models and the celebration of successful young entrepreneurs.

CESED was therefore, set up to help alleviate the challenge of unemployment among the youth, especially among graduates. The Centre was launched on 1st September 2014 to fulfil key thrust #1 and # 5 of the University's strategic plan (UCC Strategic Plan 2013–2017). Thrust #1 says the UCC would vigorously promote research, teaching and outreach that will position the University as a centre of excellence. Furthermore, thrust #5 says the University shall undertake fundraising drive by aggressively pursuing consultancy, internally generated funds and enforcing fiscal discipline.

CESED's aim is to have increasing numbers of graduates from the University, staff as well as the youth in the region, establish their own businesses and succeed in self-employment. A combination of follow-up strategies is used to help maintain the link between educational experiences and entrepreneurship practice. CESED also seeks to sustain the "German-African University partnership platform for the development of entrepreneurs and Small and Medium-Sized Enterprises" project jointly implemented by the UCC, University of Nairobi and the Bonn Rhein-Sieg University of Applied Sciences, Germany, by providing opportunities for the University and the general public at large, to gain knowledge in entrepreneurship issues.

In pursuance of this, CESED provides services such as group counselling, short seminars, mentorship and coaching for the youth in entrepreneurship. Through follow-up and counselling reports, CESED receives feedback on how acquired knowledge is being utilised and how programmes may be reviewed to make them more effective and meaningful.

Size of CESED by Staff and Role

CESED currently has five administrative staff. They are made up of the Head of Department, and three coordinators for the Business Incubator, Entrepreneurial Education and the Research and Publications Unit, respectively. There is also an Administrative Assistant, who performs the day-to-day administrative work at CESED. However, the Centre also has academic staff who help with teaching and research activities in entrepreneurship and other related disciplines. Apart from these, the business model of CESED is to draw experts from the teaching, non-teaching and industry whenever there is a project to be executed to provide counselling, mentoring and coaching of budding entrepreneurs and owners of SMEs.

CESED's Role within the University

The role of CESED is to harness innovative and viable business ideas from the young and students in institutions of higher learning and develop such ideas in business and technology incubators to shape them into products that meet the technical skills needs of industry. It also inculcates 'the can do spirit' into the young entrepreneurs and rekindles the confidence of industry in innovative corporate strategies from academia. It provides opportunity for the university and the general public at large to gain knowledge in entrepreneurship. Furthermore, CESED conducts research and develops and strengthens the entrepreneurial skills of students through training, capacity building, mentoring and coaching.

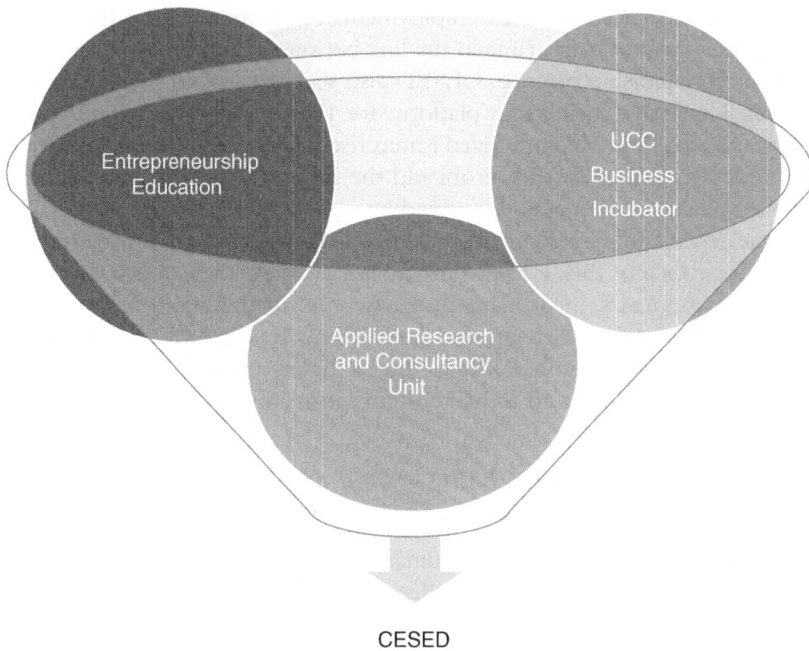

Fig. 9.1 The three interrelated activities of CESED

Services

CESED nurtures and grows business ideas, and provides business development services including mentoring and coaching. It also provides limited office space for start-ups and grant through its annual business plan competition. CESED provides its services under three interrelated subunits: entrepreneurship education, research and publications and business incubation (School of Business, 2013). Figure 9.1 provides the three core services provided by CESED.

Entrepreneurship Education

Entrepreneurship education is the fundamental activity of CESED. The role of this activity area is to facilitate the integration of entrepreneurship education into the curriculum of public and private educational institutions. Activities in this core area focus on curriculum development, innovation and production of curriculum materials. Three roles played by unit include entrepreneurship awareness programme through the introduction of university-wide undergraduate course in entrepreneurship and new venture creation. Furthermore, it is responsible for the mounting of postgraduate programmes as well as organisation of regular short courses for start-ups, entrepreneurs and small businesses. The Unit currently teaches an average of 3,000 students in every academic year, and this number is expected to increase with more departments joining. This Unit also teaches entrepreneurship courses in other institutions where such expertise is not available. For example, the Unit currently teaches at African Institute for Mathematical Sciences (AIMS) in Ghana.

Research and Publications

Research activities are the engine for creativity and innovation at CESED. The unit gathers, analyses and disseminates information that guides and supports other activities of CESED. The Unit conducts organisational audit/business diagnostics, applied organisational and marketing research as well as case studies.

The organisational and business diagnostics is a key activity of the unit. This is a comprehensive diagnostics for organisations in order to critically compare their technical and managerial expertise against best practices in order to make recommendations for improvement. This activity is conducted jointly by experts from academia and industry and in close collaboration with the client. This service is available for both SMEs and larger firms, including multinationals.

Furthermore, the applied organisational and market research focuses on needs of the businesses. In close discussion with the organisations concerned, staff and students of the UCC School of Business would design research projects in response to a specific industry problem or need. The findings would be implemented jointly by the research team and the client. This activity would also encourage both undergraduate and postgraduate students from the UCC Business School to select their research topics based on specific industry needs so that their research findings can be useful immediately. It also offers a unique opportunity for companies to also secure good research report at relatively low cost.

The applied market research activity is a consultancy service for organisations that would like to explore new markets or expand existing ones. This service is currently available for businesses that want to explore new markets in Germany, Ghana and Kenya. The research is usually conducted in close collaboration with the client and with support from our partner universities and industry partners in the respective countries. Moreover, the unit develops case studies from indigenous experiences; and develops and tests instructional materials in collaboration with the Entrepreneurship Education Unit (EEU). Furthermore, the unit evaluates programmes organised by CESED for quality assurance, and reviews, interprets and disseminates published research on entrepreneurship education to guide trainers and instructors. It also publishes newsletters, journals/magazines and books.

Through research, CESED gets enhanced insights into the nature and practice of entrepreneurship within the national and international contexts. This core activity area disseminates information through the publication of working papers, technical and research reports, journals and books.

Business Incubation

Business incubation is one of the core activities of CESED. Incubators house a staff of business professionals who can guide small firms through the difficulty of starting and growing a business. CESED through the University provides furnished office space for incubatees. This space and equipment are paid for through donations to the university. By housing many entrepreneurs in close proximity, business incubators can enable these tenants to assist one another with solutions to common problems. In addition, by providing logistical support such as floor space for offices and business development services such as coaching, training, offer of networking opportunities (that enhance access to finance, suppliers and markets), secretarial, research and other related support, business start-ups are expected to be more attractive and less daunting for novice entrepreneurs to handle.

The incubation process takes between six and twenty-four months depending on the needs of the client, and services would normally include training programmes, educational tours, coaching, mentoring, internships, business planning and other specific training required for the start-up to kickoff. The incubation unit, in collaboration with its industry partners, provides mentoring and coaching for SMEs, start-ups and young entrepreneurs to help them develop their skills and become very competitive in the market.

CESED also provides customised services for clients to suit their needs. Businesses of all kinds can contact CESED if they need any service that has not been explicitly stated and would be able to provide assistance. Sometimes, CESED would be able to play a crucial role of linking such clients to some of CESED's partners who can assist with such services at no fee. Some of the services that can also be referred to CESED are recruitment and selection; employee orientation and training; professional and legal advice; ethical training for management and employees and many others.

9.4 Business Model

The activities of CESED starts with the Research and Publications Unit (RPU). The RPU through research develops new curriculum or tailors existing ones, making it entrepreneurial focused. Moreover, with the assistance of the EEU lecturers are encouraged to change their approach to teaching and to adopt a more practiced-oriented teaching. Furthermore, through the university-wide entrepreneurship programme, facilitators try to inculcate in students the right entrepreneurial mindset. As part of the course, students are taken through opportunity identification, feasibility analysis, business planning and sourcing for grants. As part of the University of Cape Coast, University of Nairobi and the Bonn Rhein Sieg University of Applied Sciences (UCC- UoN- BRSU) joint project initiative, students who are able to write feasible business plans enter into a 'Business Plan Competition' under the project. The prizes for award are €6,000, €5,000 and €4,000 for the first, second and third positions, respectively. Since the inception of the project, about €39,000 has been awarded to about ten student start-ups from Ghana. The winners for the Business Plan Competition and other start-ups are expected to go into the business incubator for about 24 months, where they receive coaching. Moreover, since 2014 another business plan competition on renewable energy has been introduced, sponsored by the German Development Co-operation (GIZ) with €10,000 as the winning prize.

The UCC Business incubator provides business development services to these start-ups through periodic training and development programmes. Upon exit from the incubator, these start-ups are assigned mentors (experienced/successful owner-managers), who provide some free consultancy services through experience sharing with the young entrepreneur or start-up. CESED is expected to monitor the performance of these start-ups for at least five years. This is done through the submission of periodic performance reports including financial statements of the venture to CESED by

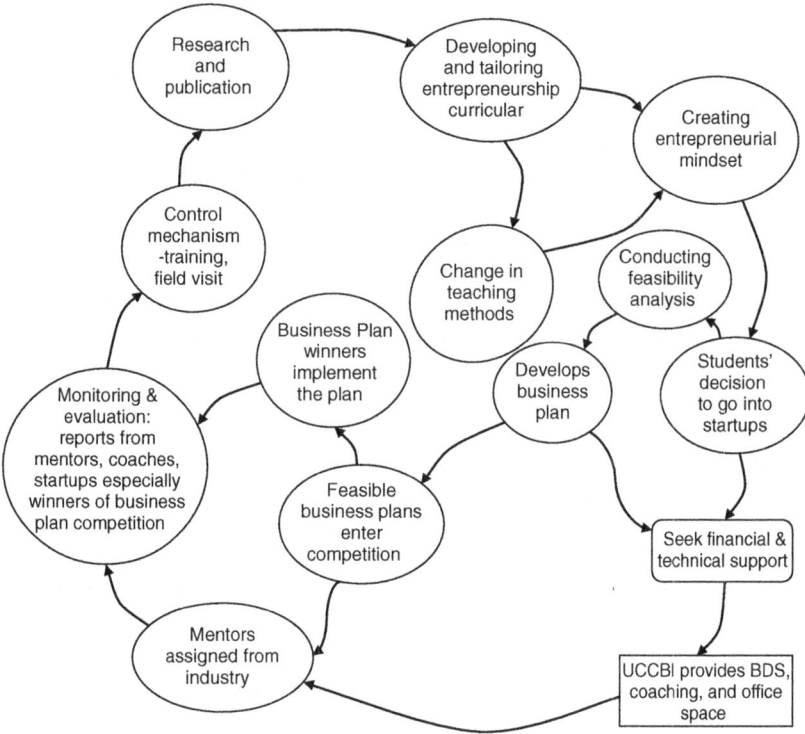

Fig. 9.2 Flow chart of activities in CESED

young entrepreneurs. The report is studied by the implementation team to enable them advice the young entrepreneur. There is also periodic site visits by a team from CESED to enable them to advice the owner/managers. Figure 9.2 is a flow chart of the activities of CESED.

CESED's ultimate aim is to have increasing numbers of graduates establish their own businesses and succeed in self-employment. A combination of follow-up strategies is used to help maintain the link between educational experiences and entrepreneurship practice. Among the services offered is group counselling, one-day seminars, scheduled visits to individuals and promotion of youth entrepreneurship association activities. Through follow-up and counselling reports, CESED receives feedback on how acquired knowledge is being utilised and how programmes may be reviewed to make them more effective.

CESED also collaborates with other consulting units within UCC including the Directorate of Research, Innovation and Consultancy and the Microfinance Unit. CESED's partners also include other private consultancy firms and individuals who have worked with CESED on previous projects and have the capacity to contribute to the implementation of similar ones in future.

9.5 Achievements

Since its inception, CESED has achieved the following successes. Firstly, CESED introduced the University-wide entrepreneurship course, which otherwise was non-existent. The course has for the past two years trained approximately 10,000 students in entrepreneurship and new venture creation. The aim of which is to encourage students to develop an entrepreneurial mindset and also think of self-employment as an alternative employment option. Secondly, in partnership with the Bonn-Rhein-Sieg University of Applied Sciences in Germany and the University of Nairobi, Kenya, CESED has organised two international joint conferences on the theme 'Teaching for Development: Platform for the Development of Entrepreneurs and Small/Medium Enterprises'. The conference has brought together academics, industry and policymakers to discuss the prospects and challenges confronting small businesses and entrepreneurs in Africa. To this end, CESED conducts marketing research for German businesses that would like to enter the Ghanaian markets and vice versa. Moreover, the aim of these conferences is to promote businesses activities between Ghanaian and German businesses. Besides, the annual business plan competitions held since 2012 have led to the setting up of 12 businesses by graduate students, thus helping solve the graduate unemployment problem in the country and also these businesses have generated several jobs and provided livelihoods in the form of income for various households.

Furthermore, in partnership with the government of Ghana and Export Trade, Agricultural & Industrial Development Fund, now EXIM Bank, CESED is currently implementing a three year project (2015–2018) the Graduate Enterprise Project Initiative. The project aims at providing both financial and technical support for graduate business initiative in agriculture and agro-processing and exports.

Other auxiliary achievements of CESED are that increasing numbers of students are becoming aware of self-employment avenues and actually enter into self-employment, instead of looking for jobs that may not be available. On average, five people walk-in into the office of CESED to make enquiries on its activities and assistance. Those who make such enquiries are typically students, staff and others in the community.

CESED has constituted a team of experienced consultants and experts from the UCC, Bonn-Rhein-Sieg University of Applied Sciences (BRSU-Germany), University of Nairobi (Kenya) and other affiliated institutions that aid in the implementation of its projects.

CESED also has a network of over 50 corporate partners mainly in Ghana who contribute to its activities in areas of providing mentoring, coaching, internships and educational trips for students and young entrepreneurs. They also partner with CESED in carrying out applied research, training of SMEs, industry exhibitions and annual stakeholders' conference.

9.6 Challenges

CESED faces several challenges. First, the host community and policy-makers are yet to fully embrace CESED and its relevance to the university's core mandate of training and developing critical skills for national development. This comes against the backdrop of the lack of awareness amongst staff and students of the critical role of entrepreneurship and its importance to institutions of higher learning. As a traditional university, which originally developed highly qualified and skilled manpower in the teaching and development of the nation's human capital, some are yet to fully embrace the concept and ideology of entrepreneurship. Certainly, this has an effect on CESED's share and portion of financial and non-financial resource distribution in the institution.

The next major challenge CESED faces is infrastructure. CESED is currently located in a limited space in one of the colleges of the university. The limited space means only few cubicles for staff and incubatees. Despite the numerous request from start-ups, the business incubator is only able to accommodate nine businesses. It is envisaged that in the future there will be a public-private partnership facility so that CESED can be funded to accommodate more incubatees.

The third issue is financial constraint. Due to the economic downturn, most donor countries and agencies have cut their budget with respect to financing such projects. Meanwhile, there is growing demand for the services provided by CESED. For example, students enrolling in the university-wide entrepreneurship course continue to increase semester by semester. This implies that more instructors for the course are required. Furthermore,

CESED would have preferred increasing the number of awards provided for the business plan competition. However, it does not have the financial flexibility to do so. Moreover, the inadequacy of funds makes it practically impossible to acquire all the logistics required for the delivery of the course.

Finally, there is inadequate staff at CESED. Moreover, the staff available require more training and skills to handle the University-wide entrepreneurship course. Although entrepreneurship as a practice is not new to the Ghanaian society, entrepreneurship education is an emerging area to her educational system. As a result of this, there is currently limited number of educators in the area of entrepreneurship. Therefore, given the number of students registering for the course, there is an urgent need to build capacity as more facilitators would be required to teach the course in the near future.

9.7 Future Development

In its 2015–2018 strategic plan, CESED is set to focus on providing entrepreneurial training for junior and senior high school students; a managerial and entrepreneurial training for vocational and technical institutions in and around its surroundings (CESED Strategic Plan 2016). It sets to provide consultancy services for SMEs through students' field visits to their businesses to help them in the areas of record-keeping, product packaging, pricing techniques and customer care. It is also set to organise boot camps, entrepreneurial clinics and expand its facility to accommodate more start-ups. It is also initiating a programme to assist lecturers and research fellows in the university to tailor their teaching/curriculum and research to make students more entrepreneurial.

9.8 Conclusion

CESED has since its inception carried out various innovative activities. Although CESED is one of the pioneers in establishing a business incubator in the country, it is yet to fully utilize its current potential due to the challenges enumerated above. The Centre has also been able to establish linkages with over 50 companies in the private sector who help young entrepreneurs go through mentoring and coaching activities. Furthermore, it adopts a multidisciplinary approach to its projects' implementation bringing together people from business, agribusiness, computer and natural sciences.

References

Centre for Entrepreneurship and Small Enterprises Development Strategic Plan (2016–2018), University of Cape Coast.

Global Employment Trend Report (2014). The risk of a jobless recovery. International Labour Organisation. http://www.ilo.org/global/research/global-reports/global-employment-trends/2014.

International Labour Office (2007). The Decent Work Agenda in Africa: 2007–2015 Retrieved on July 7, 2016 from www.ilo.org/public/english/standards/relm/rgmeet/11afrm/dg-thematic.pdf.

ISSER (2015). Worsening graduate unemployment a 'time bomb. Institute of Social Statistics and Economic Research, Accra.

Ministry of Youth and Sports. (2010). National Youth Policy for Ghana. Ministry for Youth and Sports. Retrieved from: planipolis.iiep.unesco.org/upload/Youth/Ghana/Ghana_YouthPolicy.pdf.

School of Business, University of Cape Coast (2013). Proposal for the Establishment of the Centre for Entrepreneurship and Small Enterprise Development.

University of Cape Coast Act, 1971 (Act 390).

University of Cape Coast Strategic Plan (2013–2017).

University of Cape Coast Law (1992) (PNDC Law 278).

World Bank (2016). Landscape of Jobs in Ghana. Retrieved from: http://www.ghanatrade.gov.gh/Trade-News/48-ghanaian-youth-jobless-world-bank.html.

Rosemond Boohene is an Associate Professor in Entrepreneurship and Small Enterprise Development at the School of Business, University of Cape Coast. She has over the years consulted and written proposals for the Cape Coast Chamber of Commerce and Industry and the Cape Coast Association of Garages to secure funding from the Council for Vocational Technical Education (COTVET). Currently, she is managing a project on Entrepreneurship and Sustainable Economic Development – a collaboration between the School of Business, University of Cape Coast, University of Nairobi and the Bonn-Rhein-Sieg, University of Applied Sciences, Germany. Other projects she is currently implementing include the Graduate Enterprise Development Initiative project by the EXIM Bank of Ghana and an European Union/United Nations Environmental Programme Project dubbed Switch Africa Green project.

Daniel Agyapong is a Senior Lecturer in Finance and Entrepreneurship and the Head, Department of Marketing and Supply Chain Managements at the School of Business, University of Cape Coast. He is also a youth and micro-, small- and medium-enterprise development consultant. Through his consultancy work, he has written several business proposals for the University and organisations such as the Ghana Heritage Conservation Trust. Other business proposals developed with colleagues from the School of Business include University of Cape Coast School of Medical Sciences Diagnostic Centre, Department of Laboratory Technology Production of Detergent, University Community Basic School Complex, and the business plan for the establishment of University of Cape Coast Transport and Auto Services Centre. Moreover, he currently manages an international cross-cultural project dubbed 'Business Bridge' between students from Germany, Ghana and Kenya as part of the University of Cape Coast and the Bonn-Rhein-Sieg, University of Applied Sciences, Germany, partnership. He is an Associate Member of the Chartered Institute of Marketing (UK).

PART IV

Guidelines for Maintaining Sustainable Entrepreneurship Centres

This last section of the book focuses on guidelines and process questions that can assist in building and maintaining dynamic entrepreneurship centres.

CHAPTER 10

Guidelines for Maintaining Sustainable Entrepreneurial Centres

Gideon Maas and Paul Jones

Abstract Regional differences determine the way entrepreneurship centres should be organised stimulating socio-economic development. Therefore, a general approach to organising entrepreneurship centres cannot be created. In this chapter, the focus is on providing background on important criteria improving the sustainability of entrepreneurship centres, supported by various process questions that can assist such centres to make a dynamic contribution to socio-economic development.

Keywords Sustainability · Successful development · Strategy · Geographical provision · Resourcing · Curriculum

10.1 Introduction

Although there are various debates around entrepreneurship centres and the way they operate, the university location and staffing of these centres do play an important role in promoting the enterprise and

G. Maas (✉) · P. Jones
International Centre for Transformational Entrepreneurship, Coventry University, Coventry, United Kingdom
e-mail: gmaas@coventry.ac.uk; ac0359@coventry.ac.uk

© The Author(s) 2017
G. Maas, P. Jones (eds.), *Entrepreneurship Centres*,
DOI 10.1007/978-3-319-47892-0_10

entrepreneurship agenda within a higher education institution. Certain institutional boundaries force some entrepreneurship centres to focus on survival rather than making a dynamic contribution to internal and external regional challenges. The question can therefore be raised whether all entrepreneurship centres are promoting the enterprise and entrepreneurship agenda effectively and whether they make a substantial contribution to transformational entrepreneurship. The focus of this book is on transformational entrepreneurship (promoting sustainable socio-economic development) rather than on a dynamic microenterprise orientation. This chapter concludes on lessons learnt from the cases discussed in the previous chapters, combine that with criteria for transformational entrepreneurship and provide guidelines on how to proceed building the enterprise and entrepreneurship agenda through dynamic entrepreneurship centres.

10.2 Guidelines for Entrepreneurship Centres

This section focuses on what the authors regard as the most important guidelines that should be addressed to create and maintain a successful entrepreneurship centre. It is not a how-to guide because regional and national differences need to be taken into consideration when strategies for entrepreneurship centres are created. The general guidelines are discussed in the following paragraphs and then stated as questions in Table 10.1.

Corporate Strategy

From literature and the cases presented, it is clear that a dynamic corporate strategy is required guiding enterprise and entrepreneurial activities within higher education institutions (HEIs). Enterprise and entrepreneurial activities cannot act in isolation neither can it be regarded as merely ad-on functions of HEIs. The HEI's specific strategy for enterprise and entrepreneurship should be in line with regional and global realities and supportive of an entrepreneurial ecosystem in that region. The authors discovered in their research that not all entrepreneurship centres agree that they know what their HEI's enterprise and entrepreneurship strategy is and that enterprise and entrepreneurship activities are often fragmented and disconnected across the HEI. The question is whom do you call when you want to know something about enterprise and entrepreneurship within a HEI? Furthermore, a more focused

Table 10.1 Guiding questions for entrepreneurship centres

Category	Questions
Corporate strategy	• Is enterprise and entrepreneurship included in the HEI's corporate strategy? • Is there a clear operational strategy for enterprise and entrepreneurship? • Is there a transparent focus for transformational entrepreneurship within the HEI? • Is there an internal transformational entrepreneurial ecosystem in the HEI? • Is there an external transformational entrepreneurial ecosystem in the region? • Is there a dedicated point of contact for all enterprise and entrepreneurship queries in the HEI? • Is there a regional narrative promoting transformational entrepreneurship?
Entrepreneurship centre's vision and strategy	• Is the transformational purpose of the centre clear? • Is the vision focusing on improving sustainable socio-economic development? • Do the vision and strategy fit in with the operational enterprise and entrepreneurship strategy of the institution?
Geographical provision of services	• What is the primary geographical focus of the entrepreneurship centre? • If the centre focuses on the global market, is the rationale for that involvement spelled out clearly?
Resourcing entrepreneurship centres	• Is it agreed whether the centre is a cost centre, a net income contribution centre or a hybrid between those two approaches? • Is there a five year budget allowing for the scalability of the centre's activities? • Are promotion lines for staff spelled out clearly? • Does the centre have support to obtain additional resources? • Are the financial sources supporting a sustainable centre?
Curriculum involvement	• Are there specific modules/programmes promoting enterprise and entrepreneurship? • Does the centre organise staff development workshops for all faculties focusing on enterprise and entrepreneurship matters? • Are all curriculum related to enterprise and entrepreneurship reviewed on a regular basis in terms of their transformational focus?

(*continued*)

Table 10.1 (continued)

Category	Questions
Co-curricular/ extracurricular involvement	• Is their a recognition system in place for students involvement in extracurricular activities? • Is there a menu of activities in which students can participate improving their understanding and skills regarding enterprise and entrepreneurship? • Who are the main partners promoting extracurricular activities within a HEI? • Is the centre monitoring and controlling all extracurricular activities?
Research involvement	• Are there agreed themes to be researched? • Are these themes in line with the transformational entrepreneurial drive of the institution? • Does a doctoral academy exist? • Are there frequent exchanges of research info? • Are research results visible to all stakeholders?
Governance and location	• Is there an independent/neutral home for the centre in the institution? • Is there an institutional committee that supports the enterprise and entrepreneurship agenda within the institution? • Are there specific criteria measuring the effectiveness of the centre?
Staffing	• Are there adequate staff members to address the vision and strategies of the centre? • Is there a succession plan in place for the director and senior staff of the centre?
National networking	• Does the centre get involved in external networking events focusing on enterprise and entrepreneurship matters?

approach promoting transformational entrepreneurship (within the context of contextual differences) among entrepreneurship centres might assist the support of entrepreneurial ecosystems and socio-economic growth far more effectively than a uniform approach among entrepreneurship centres.

Entrepreneurship Centre's Vision and Strategy

The relationship between education, research and business engagement is a central theme from all cases. However, differences are observed in the different vision statements of the entrepreneurship centres. In some cases, they focus on the external environment such as socio-economic development whilst others on becoming the leader in entrepreneurship education and research. The validity of both approaches cannot be negated – however, in a transformational context, it can be argued that the focus should be on the impact the centres make to stimulate socio-economic growth. There is nothing wrong with seeking to become the leader in the field of entrepreneurship education but it is regarded as secondary rather than the primary purpose of an entrepreneurship centre stimulating transformational entrepreneurship. From the author's research, it is apparent that the centre's strategies should revolve around education provision, research and business support. Other variances of the centre's strategies include a focus on survival, blending theory and practice in a meaningful manner, creating a single brand for enterprise and entrepreneurship activities at the HEI, and improving student experience. The test of a good entrepreneurship centre strategy would therefore be determined by the degree of fit with the HEIs corporate strategy and how it is connected with regional realities. Therefore, HEIs should invest time and resources to create viable and visible enterprise and entrepreneurship strategies and link these strategies to entrepreneurial ecosystems in their specific regions.

Geographical Provision of Services

The geographical regions in which entrepreneurship centres operate include local, regional and transnational areas. Although centres argued that their geographical spread is determined by the demand for their services, they also mentioned a challenging environment regarding resources. Therefore, a clearer rationale should be provided by HEIs why their entrepreneurship centres should undertake their activities beyond the regional domain. There is nothing wrong with operating internationally as long as it is linked to the HEI's corporate strategy for enterprise and entrepreneurship. The rationale should be on transformational entrepreneurship and how it can assist socio-economic development and not only creating reputational gains for the HEI. In terms of services, the entrepreneurship centres perform a wide spectrum of activities from curriculum design and implementation to assistance with small business start-ups. From this, one can argue that the range of activities is too wide and can be performed by other actors, for example, business start-ups by technology parks.

Resourcing Entrepreneurship Centres

Entrepreneurship centres are funded from various resources such as grants, industry contracts, internal funding, research and teaching income. A combination of these sources is used to ensure centre sustainability and these centres proudly referred to their financial contributions to their university's central budget. Although the resourcing model works, the pressure is with regard to scalability of the centre's activities and obtaining the optimum balance between intra- and extracurricular activity. This debate surrounding resources brings into question the social investment of HEIs into socio-economic growth. Obtaining funding from external sources alone and which is normally project focused can take resources away from the real purpose of an entrepreneurship centre. Within an environment of restricted funding the importance of being financially viable is not negated – a more optimal balance between internal and external financial sources is argued for especially if entrepreneurship centres are to become more involved in longer-term research projects. HEIs and government should investigate the availability of longer-term financial resources for entrepreneurship centres.

Curriculum Involvement

Entrepreneurship centres are involved in leading curriculum design, presenting specific programmes and supporting curriculum delivery. When analysing the future role of centres in the provision of curriculum, it is apparent that centres should fulfil a champion's role in curriculum development and support implementation of curriculum across faculties in a HEI.

Co-Curricular/Extracurricular Involvement

When analysing the future role of centres in the provision of co-curricular/extracurricular activities, three areas of involvement are important, namely improved engagement with community, maintaining contact with students and alumni, and providing across university services. However, the staff and infrastructure required for this is different from those needed for typical university teaching and research activities. Therefore, consideration should be given to have separate divisions within a centre addressing the different focus areas or delegate this activity to another role player within the HEI's entrepreneurial ecosystem, for example, technoparks.

Research Involvement

One area that seems to be under pressure in many entrepreneurship centres is research and policy formulation. From research, it is clear that senior managers expect an improved focus on research and policy – in the UK driven by benchmarking exercises such as the Research Evaluation Framework formulation. Such activities might support the operation of entrepreneurial ecosystems to be longer term orientated than the relative short-termism of five years (i.e. the length between elections and the formation of a new government). Entrepreneurship centres should therefore develop a unique focus area for their research in relation to transformational entrepreneurship, for example, the role of entrepreneurial leadership, innovation and entrepreneurial education within transformational entrepreneurship. Cross-cutting themes such as a focus on socioeconomic development, policy and practice matters should support these specific focus areas. The focus of activities can be on local and global areas. Benefits from established networks locally [e.g. through involvement in learned societies such as the Institute of Small Business and Entrepreneurship and within specific continents (e.g. Africa Institute for Transformational Entrepreneurship)] should be explored. In general, validation of a centre's research activity can occur through various channels such as the Research Excellence Framework in the UK, development of young researchers, creation of case studies that can highlight real-life cases in transformational entrepreneurship, undertaking transnational research projects and building up of a PhD community to encourage accelerated research in specific themes.

Governance and Location

Entrepreneurship centres are using various methods of governance such as Advisory Boards, Management Boards and functioning independently from faculties or being part of a specific faculty. It seems that decisions regarding governance are mostly influenced by financial constraints or a leading figure in the HEI than derived from the corporate strategy. Thus it is not surprising that research indicates mixed results in terms of the involvement of boards, committees or where entrepreneurship centres are located. Enterprise and entrepreneurship are multidisciplinary concepts that are not for the domain of a specific faculty alone because internal political barriers might exist if such a centre belongs to a specific faculty.

Location of entrepreneurship centres should therefore allow them to operate freely among all units within a HEI and with relevant external stakeholders.

Staffing

Staffing is a concern to many entrepreneurship centres in terms of availability and promotion. The route to promotion for staff members in entrepreneurship centres is often unclear and difficult to achieve if traditional practices to promotion (e.g. publications in ABS-ranked journals) are overshadowing with what skills, experience and deliverables are required from staff members in entrepreneurship centres. HEIs should investigate the route to promotion for staff members within entrepreneurship centres – a different category of professorship can probably go a long way addressing this point.

National Networking

When researching this book, the authors realised that although staff members of entrepreneurship centres are in contact with one another they seldom meet as a group to discuss matters of mutual concern. Neither do they reflect on future potential activities and best practices from the various entrepreneurship centres. Therefore, annual gatherings of entrepreneurship centres within a specific region might be a starting point to achieve a more focused approach on transformational entrepreneurship.

10.3 STAYING RELEVANT AND INNOVATIVE

This section focuses on various questions that new or even existing entrepreneurship centres can ask themselves in order to stay relevant and innovative.

10.4 CONCLUSION

The world is and will still be going through rapid changes in the future and will influence the way entrepreneurship centres organise themselves. Through the right investments in vision, strategy, resources and skills of staff, entrepreneurship centres should be able to stay in a floating equilibrium with these changes and still make a dynamic impact on socio-economic development through transformational practices. What is for sure is that entrepreneurship centres cannot proceed on traditional paths that typically have limited internal or external impact.

Gideon Maas is the Director of the International Centre for Transformational Entrepreneurship and Professor of Professional Practice at Coventry University, UK. Gideon has broad international business and academic experiences in various countries. Within the academic environment, Gideon has created various entrepreneurship centres at different universities over the past years, developed and implemented undergraduate and postgraduate modules and programmes focusing specifically on enterprise and entrepreneurship. Recently, Gideon has created the Africa Institute for Transformational Entrepreneurship to assist African countries in supporting sustainable socio-economic growth. Gideon's research focus and experiences are in entrepreneurship, open innovation, growth strategies, entrepreneurial universities, implementation of entrepreneurial systems and family businesses. His research activities are industry and academic related, and he has published various books and articles in the public domain. Gideon is also currently a Visiting Professor at Anglia-Ruskin University and Vice President (Policy and Practice) of the Board of Trustees of the Institute of Small Business and Entrepreneurship.

Paul Jones is the Deputy Director of the International Centre for Transformational Entrepreneurship and Professor in Entrepreneurship at Coventry University. Prof Jones has worked in further and higher education for over 25 years. Prof Jones is an active researcher in the entrepreneurship discipline with 200-plus outputs including edited books (1), academic journals (49), book chapters (5), conference papers (103), working papers (11), reports (2) and research monographs (1) since 2002. Prof Jones is currently Editor-in-Chief of the *International Journal of Entrepreneurial Behaviour and Research* and Associate Editor of the *International Journal of Management Education*. In addition, Prof Jones has acted as a Guest Editor for several special issues including a special edition of the *Journal of Systems and Information Technology* examining the usage and impact of E-Business within the small business sector. In 2013, he was a Guest Editor for a special edition of the *Journal of Small Business and Enterprise Development* exploring international deployment examples of E-Business. In 2014, he acted as a Guest Editor for a special edition of *Education + Training* investigating the impact of e-learning and also as a Guest Editor for a special edition of the *International Journal of Management Education* exploring Entrepreneurial Education and its ability to implement change.

Index

B
Babson College, 84, 101, 102
Business School, 13, 29, 30, 37, 38, 42, 44, 49, 50, 53, 62, 65, 67, 68, 70–72, 79, 81–94, 102, 106, 112–120, 131

C
Co-curricular/extra-curricular, 84, 92, 148
Corporate Strategy, 13–15, 79, 144–147, 149
Coventry University (UK)
  Add+Vantage, 23–24, 27–28
  BA in Enterprise and Entrepreneurship, 24, 27, 29–33
  Business Development Support Office (BDSO), 23
  Business Enterprise Support Team (BEST), 23, 27
  Coventry University College, 20, 21
  Coventry University Enterprises (CUE), 21–24, 26, 34
  Coventry University London Campus (CULC), 21
  Institute of Applied Entrepreneurship (IAE), 19–26
  International Centre for Transformational Entrepreneurship (ICTE), 20, 26, 27, 29, 34–38
  Latham, John, 21
  MA in Enterprise and Entrepreneurship Education, 27, 35–36
  MA in Global Entrepreneurship, 27, 32
  Student Enterprise Centre (SEC), 23

E
Economic and Social Research Council (ESRC), 43, 50
EDEM Business School (Spain)
  Angels Investment Society, 82
  BBA in Entrepreneurship, 84
  BSc in Engineering and Management, 84, 87
  Cross-curricular project, 87–90
  Lanzadera accelerator, 82, 84
  Marina de Empresas (MdE), 82, 85

EDEM Business School (Spain) (*cont.*)
  Valencian Business Association
    (AVE), 82
Enterprise, 5, 6, 8, 12–14, 19–20,
  22–24, 27, 29, 30–32, 35, 37, 43,
  48, 49, 52, 64–65, 67, 71–72,
  127–133, 144, 147, 149
Entrepreneurial eco-system, 5, 6, 8, 69
Entrepreneurial University, 6, 12, 13,
  20, 23, 38, 47
Entrepreneurship, 3–8, 11–15, 20,
  22–26, 31, 32–37, 42, 44–50, 52,
  61–72, 84–87, 97–109,
  111–122, 125–137,
  144–150
Entrepreneurship Centre, 4, 6, 11–15,
  20, 22, 72, 97–109, 117,
  143–150
European Regional Development
  Fund (ERDF), 43, 55
European Union, 5, 42–44
European Union, Northwest Regional
  Development Agency
  (NWDA), 42

G
Geographical provision, 147
Global Entrepreneurship Monitor
  (GEM), 107, 115
  National Survey of Experts
    (NES), 107
Governance and location, 149–150

H
Higher Education Innovation Fund
  (HEIF), 42
Higher Education Institutions
  (HEI), 4, 6, 12–15, 36, 62, 144,
  147–150

Hunter Centre for Entrepreneurship
  and Innovation (HCEI)
  (Canada), 111–122
  Cannon, Elizabeth, 113
  Centre for Employment,
    Competitiveness and Growth
    (ECG), Kent University, 121
  Energy New Venture
    Competition, 119
  Fast Pitch Competition, 119
  University of Calgary, 112

I
Innovation, 4, 5, 6, 8, 20, 23, 24, 35,
  42–45, 48, 49, 52, 55, 56, 69, 89,
  90, 93, 94, 98, 99, 101,
  104–106, 108, 111–122, 131,
  135, 149

L
Lancaster University (UK)
  Bachelor degree in Management
    and Entrepreneurship, 47
  Berkeley Innovation Forum
    (BIF), 44, 56
  Daresbury Science and Innovation
    Campus (DSIC), 52
  Department for Entrepreneurship,
    Strategy and Innovation
    (DESI), 42–52
  Entrepreneurs-in-Residence, 47, 51
  European Masters in
    Management, 49
  Innovation, Design,
    Entrepreneurship and Science
    (IDEAS), 52
  Institute for Entrepreneurship and
    Enterprise Development
    (IEED), 42, 44, 45

INDEX 155

Knowledge Acceleration and Responsible Innovation Meta-network (KARIM), 44, 56
Lancashire and Cumbria Regional Growth programmes for SMEs, 51
Lancaster China Catalyst Programme (LCCP), 44, 56–57
Lancaster University Management School (LUMS), 42–44, 46, 47, 50, 52, 53, 55, 56
LEAD 2 Innovate, 55
London Creative and Digital Fusion Project, 55–56
MSc in Entrepreneurship, Innovation and Practice, 48, 49
MSc in International Innovation (Entrepreneurship), 48
Nano Regions Alliance (NANORA), 44
North West of England, 44, 47, 52
PhD, 47, 49
The Small Business Charter award, 44
Wave 2 Growth Hubs (W2GH), 43, 52–53

M
Micro-business, 7

N
Networks, 48, 49, 52, 57, 71, 108, 149

R
Regional Growth Fund (RGF), 43, 52–53
Relevance, 30, 136
Research, 6, 12, 13, 14, 20, 21, 23, 24, 26, 31, 42–44, 45–47, 49–50, 52, 53, 62–72, 84, 100–102, 106, 107–108, 112, 113, 115, 116, 118–121, 126, 128, 129–133, 135–137, 144, 146–149
Research Assessment Exercise (RAE), 70
Research Evaluation Framework (REF), 67, 70–72, 149
Resourcing, 148

S
Santander International Entrepreneurship Centre (CISE)
Entrepreneurship program (DOCE), 106
E2 programme, 103, 107
Escuela de Organización Industrial (EOI), 102, 104, 106
Organization of Ibero-American States (OEI), 102
Organization of Spanish University Rectors (CRUE), 102
University of Cantabria (UC), 97–109
YUZZ, 105–108
Scottish Centres-for-Entrepreneurship
Aberdeen University, 63, 64, 66, 67
Edinburgh University, 66
Heriot Watt University, 66
Hunter Centre, 64, 66, 73
Paisley Entrepreneurship Research Centre (PERC), 66
Robert Gordon University, 64
Scottish Institute for Enterprise (SIE), 64
Scottish Programme for Entrepreneurship (SPE), 64
Scottish School, 62, 63, 69, 71–72
Scottish School of Entrepreneurship (SER), 62

Scottish Centres-for-Entrepreneurship (*cont.*)
  Stirling University, 64–66
  Strathclyde University, 64, 66
Small and Medium Sized Enterprise (SME), 22, 42, 44, 50, 51, 53, 55, 56, 106, 115, 126
Social Entrepreneurship, 4, 27
Socio-Economic development, 4, 27
Socio-Economic Growth, 5, 7, 8, 12, 37, 146–148
Staffing, 30, 143, 150
Systemic Entrepreneurship, 5

T
Total early-stage Entrepreneurial Activity (TEA), 99
Transformational Entrepreneurship, 5, 7–8, 12, 20, 26, 36–37, 144, 146, 147, 149, 150

U
United Kingdom, 5
University of Cape Coast (UCC) (Ghana), 125–137

African Institute for Mathematical Sciences (AIMS), 131
Bonn-Rhein-Sieg University of Applied Sciences (BRSU) (Germany), 127, 133, 135, 136
Bundesministerium Für Wirtschaftliche Zusammenarbeit (BMZ), 127
Centre for Entrepreneurship and Small Enterprises Development (CESED), 126–137
Deutscher Akademischer Austauschdienst (DAAD), 127
Export Trade, Agricultural & Industrial Development Fund (EDAIF), 135
Ghana National Chamber of Commerce, 127
Research and Publications Unit (RPU), 129, 133
University of Cape Coast Business incubator (UCCBI), 133

W
World Economic Forum, 21–22

The manufacturer's authorised representative in the EU is Springer Nature Customer Service Centre GmbH, Europaplatz 3, 69115 Heidelberg, Germany. If you have any concerns regarding our products, please contact ProductSafety@springernature.com

Printed and bound by CPI Group (UK) Ltd, Croydon, CR0 4YY
23/03/2026
02076402-0012